The
SELF-
COACHED
RUNNER

The
SELF-
COACHED
RUNNER

By Allan Lawrence
and Mark Scheid

With a Foreword by Pat Clohessy,
Australian National Coach — Distance Running

LITTLE, BROWN AND COMPANY • BOSTON • TORONTO

Second Printing

D

Before embarking on any strenuous exercise program, including
the training described in this book, everyone, particularly anyone with any known heart or blood-pressure problem, should
be examined by a physician.

LIBRARY OF CONGRESS CATALOGING IN PUBLICATION DATA

Lawrence, Allan.
 The self-coached runner.

 Includes index.
 1. Running. I. Scheid, Mark. II. Title.
 GV1 61.L33 1984 796.4'26 84-7934
 ISBN 0-316-51671-6 (pbk.)
 ISBN 0-316-51672-4

MV

DESIGNED BY DEDE CUMMINGS

*Published simultaneously in Canada
by Little, Brown & Company (Canada) Limited*

PRINTED IN THE UNITED STATES OF AMERICA

For Mary

— M.S.

To my father, George, for his love, encouragement, and unwavering support in the first ten barren years of my competitive running, in particular, and then throughout my career

To Cecil "Chicks" Hensley, my first coach and lifetime friend, who patiently taught me the "art" of running and showed me that the "best-trained mug in the world" could make it in distance running

To John W. Morriss, former head track coach at the University of Houston, who taught me how to evaluate and strengthen my own psychological weaknesses and "read" the same weaknesses in opponents

To Wilber "Boss" Maxwell, my American "father," who, unfortunately, never lived to see this book a reality

my sincere appreciation, profound respect — and love.

— A.L.

ACKNOWLEDGMENTS

WE WOULD LIKE TO THANK a number of people who read and commented upon the manuscript of *The Self-Coached Runner*: Barrie Almond, Pat Clohessy, Mary Cullen, Roy Cullen, Bruce Glikin, Bredo Johnsen, Diane Thomas, Lynn Trafton, and Dr. Bernie Finch.

The ideas which underlie the treatment of running injuries came primarily from Dr. Donald Baxter. Special thanks are due to Dr. Herbert L. Fred, multiple ultra-marathon record holder, for his incisive comments on matters medical and stylistic.

Lynn Trafton took many of the pictures used in the book, and literally made the book possible by her gift to the senior author — a typewriter.

Jane Butler retyped much of the final manuscript quickly and accurately. Mary Scheid read and corrected drafts, suggested changes in wording, organization, and format, and edited and re-edited almost every word.

At Little, Brown and Company, we would especially like to thank Ray Roberts for his timely advice. To Ann Sleeper go our thanks for her suggestions, and our hopes that this book will help her running as much as she improved this book.

A. L. AND M. S.
HOUSTON, TEXAS

CONTENTS

You and This Book

THIS BOOK IS WRITTEN for the runner who coaches himself or herself. Because of this orientation, it differs in several ways from other running books. Instead of assuming that all runners are the same and need the same type of training — or, alternatively, lumping all runners into hopelessly large groups (all who run a marathon in anywhere from 2 hours 40 minutes to 3 hours 10 minutes, for example) — this book provides specific individualized schedules for many different time goals at three distances: the 10K, the various races around 10 miles in length (15K, 10-mile, 20K, ½-marathon), and the marathon. It also provides guidelines to tell you whether you are ready to train for the time you hope to run.

In addition to providing you with the information you need to improve your running, and detailed day-by-day schedules to enable you to do so, *The Self-Coached Runner* provides you with the background information you need to coach yourself. The first chapter deals with the typical problems self-coached runners have, and how to overcome them. The second chapter gives the philosophy behind each workout in your schedule — not only what you are doing on a given day, but why and how each training run fits into your overall improvement. Chapter 3 deals with correct running form and how to attain the aspects of it which matter, including "mental form." The fourth chapter deals with injuries

— how to avoid them, what to do if you get them anyway, when to see a doctor and what kind of doctor to see, and what to do during and after recovery. Chapter 5 teaches you how to compete, and Chapter 6 shows you how to recover from competition. The actual training schedules make up Chapter 7. They range from 30 minutes to 55 minutes for the 10K, from 50 minutes to 90 minutes for the approximately 10-mile distances, and from 2 hours 20 minutes to a "survival" marathon of 5 hours.

The last chapter, "Backgrounds," provides information of special use to the runner who is just beginning to get involved in competition.

Because it is the first book written for the self-coached runner, this book is designed to act in some ways as your coach. Like a coach, it provides guidelines to help you set reasonable and achievable goals. Like a coach, it tells you how to train and how to compete, when to make workouts tougher and when to ease up, when to pace and when to race.

It provides specific day-to-day workouts scaled to your ability and designed to lead you to higher levels, and puts them in an explicit philosophy of coaching so that you can understand the reasons behind each workout.

Most of all, this book trains you to coach yourself, so that your ability to improve will not depend upon chance, upon your running buddies or the competition, or even upon this book.

It will depend upon you — the self-coached runner.

FOREWORD

ALLAN LAWRENCE IS UNIQUELY QUALIFIED to write a book on running. He has been a student of distance running in Australia and the United States since the mid-1950s; and he was one of the most versatile distance runners in his era.

Allan won a bronze medal in the 1956 Melbourne Olympics, in the 10,000 meters. He excelled on the track and also in cross-country, where he was the only male runner to win both the NCAA (National Collegiate Athletic Association) and AAU (Amateur Athletic Union) — now TAC (The Athletics Congress of the United States) — in one year. Allan also set indoor world records at 2 miles and 3 miles.

This high-quality versatility was the result of a rare dedication, common sense, and studied application to best cope with the specific requirements of each type of running.

Allan describes himself as an average runner who has been exceptionally well trained. This sensitivity and knowledge of himself and how such a runner could attain excellence enable Allan to appreciate the needs of all and steer them along the road to satisfactory improvement.

Allan always has had a generous interest in people. I recall his encouragement to me when I was a rising young runner in Muswellbrook and Tamworth, Australia, and later when his advice was so decisive at Nationals in the United States. He was thrilled to see my improvement, even if it meant occasional wins at his own expense.* He saw potential in others and encouraged it, and I know of hundreds in Australia and the United States from Olympic pentathlon athletes to business men and women who have benefited greatly from Allan's advice.

He has always shown a rare appreciation of an individual's needs, and his methods were always "safe" and designed to meet specific needs. No modest ambition is too small for Allan's interest and attention. I think this quality is as unique as his versatile record of excellence.

Indeed, this book is a timely contribution to community fitness and to the popular running explosion at all levels, not only in the United States but wherever aspiring runners are searching for a satisfying interest and for continued improvement.

I commend this book to all runners.

PAT CLOHESSY
AUSTRALIAN NATIONAL COACH,
DISTANCE RUNNING
OLYMPIC COACH,
1984, LOS ANGELES

*Clohessy succeeded Lawrence as NCAA Champion in 1961 and 1962.

ONE

The Self-
Coached Runner

SUNDAY, OCTOBER 11, 1964, TOKYO, JAPAN. It is the second day of the Tokyo Olympics, three days before the finals of the Olympic 10,000-meter run.

At dusk, Ron Clarke of Australia jogs onto the training track. Clarke, the world-record holder at 10,000 meters and eight other distances, is the overwhelming favorite to take the gold medal in the Olympic final. This is to be his last easy workout before the race.

But as Clarke moves easily around the track, his strides begin to lengthen, his pace quickens, and he runs faster and faster. One by one, the other Olympic athletes on the track stop to watch the workout of the world's greatest distance runner. Caught up in the rhythm of the run, and impelled by years of training and his great physical strength, Clarke continues to increase his pace. His first mile is fast; the second is faster; 5000 meters comes up in world-class time. At four miles, the watches of bystanders record an unofficial world record.

Clarke, heedless of his upcoming race and intoxicated with the speed and rhythm he has established, holds his pace for another half-mile. Then at last responding to the pleas of several other Australian runners at trackside, he slows, jogs off the track, and ends his workout.

But the damage is done: three days later in the Olympic final, Clarke is third — an outstanding accomplishment, but far below the expectations of the track world, and of Clarke himself.

When Ron Clarke told me about this incident, my first response was, "Why?"

"I don't know, Al. I felt compelled, and I felt very good. I just wanted to test my fitness." (Clarke, in fact, often ran world-class times in training. Even today he recalls his four-mile time trial on the Olympic track as "Okay — but nothing special.")

I didn't ask where his coach had been during his suicidal workout. I knew he had been self-coached for years.

If you are a self-coached runner, you've probably been in Clarke's shoes: you have trained weeks and months for a certain race, only to have your performance fall far below your expectations.

You can't understand what happened. Usually you spend the next few easy runs recovering from the race and trying to analyze your problem. It's not lack of training — your workouts have gone okay; some, in fact, have been excellent. It can't be ignorance, either — you've read most of the books. You know how to pick shoes, how to stretch, what to eat, when to drink, and even what to wear.

As you go over the possible causes of your poor performance and dismiss them one by one, you eventually come down to the runner's traditional last resort: "I guess I just had a bad day."

Maybe you did.

But if you think you have "bad days" — seemingly chance or random variations in your running ability that cause you to perform far below your usual level — ask yourself these questions:

• Do you have as many "good days" as "bad days"? (If it is really random, you should be surpassing your usual level as often as you fall below it.)

• Do the better runners seem to have as many bad days as you do? (If it's chance, it should affect all runners.)

In fact, what is commonly called a bad day affects nearly all sub-elite runners (but very few of the elite), and it is almost never offset by a surprisingly good performance.

It's not a bad day. What is your problem, then?

Your problem is one shared by tens of thousands of your fellow runners throughout the world: in spite of knowing nearly everything you need to know about running theories, you lack an organizing principle to put everything into perspective.

You are the Self-Coached Runner. And you didn't have a bad day; you had a bad coach. That's the difference between you and the elite.

Before you can become a better runner, you're going to need to become a better coach. That's what this chapter is about.

Common Mistakes of Self-Coached Athletes

If you coach yourself, you will probably recognize one or more of these in yourself.

1. *Mixed Philosophies of Training.* One of the results of the running boom is that a number of publications have made the average runner much more sophisticated about training theories than the most knowledgeable coach of twenty years ago. The average runner today has read article after article on long, slow distance training, interval training, hill training, Lydiard training, Dellinger training, Viren training, fartlek training, beach training, track training, road training, and running in place. This, of course, is in addition to cross-training with weights, bicycles, jumpropes, altitude simulators, and swimming, and in conjunction with chiropractic, yoga, massage, rolfing, fasting, carbo-loading, and the Pritikin diet.

It is no wonder that, when you run a poor race, you ask yourself, "Do I need a little more ——— ?" and fill in the blank with whatever type of training got the most ink in a recent issue of *Runner* or *Runner's World*.

And in fact one of these training tips may be just what you need. But the odds are against it. And when you start mixing components from different training philosophies, you are very likely to have too much of one ingredient and not enough of three or four.

2. *Doing Other Runners' Workouts.* A related problem can occur two different ways, with equally destructive results.

Perhaps you ask a local hotshot what kind of training he does. "Twenty times a quarter all out, with a one-minute recovery, twice a week," he says. "Just jog the rest of the time." That may be right for him, but it will very likely leave you unable to do another workout for a week or two. Different runners need different workouts, workouts suited to their strengths and weaknesses.

This problem can also occur almost unconsciously. You decide as you're driving over to the track that you need to do 3 × a mile with a quarter jog — it's a tough workout, but you think it might set you up just right for the ten-kilometer (10K) in two weeks. When you get to the track, though, you meet one of your running buddies who has decided that 16 × 220 is what she needs. She invites you to sit in.*

"What the hell," you think. "It'll probably do me good, and it's a lot more fun to run with somebody." It might be what you need, all right. But if it is, why did you decide to run the mile workout?

3. *Failure to Set a Schedule.* The reason you were so easily persuaded to run someone else's workout was that you didn't really believe you needed to run repeat miles anyway — you just thought that up on the way to the track. You assume that your buddy has spent some conscious effort to come up with her workout, and that she has a good reason for running it. Maybe she has, and maybe *she* just thought it up on *her* way to the track. In any case, what she needs is not necessarily what you need.

4. *Doing the Workouts You Do Well.* If you're setting your own schedule, notice how often you do those workouts which impress yourself. "I must be in pretty good shape — I just went through ten miles in sixty-two minutes and it didn't feel that bad." Next week you'll shoot for 61 minutes, and the week after that . . . In the meantime, you will tend to ignore workouts that seem to be harder work for slower times. This is nature's way of telling you that you need to work in *that* area, not the one where you're already doing well.

5. *Doing Workouts that Impress Others.* A similar problem usually occurs at one end of the running spectrum or the other: fast and short, or long and slow. These workouts are not easy (unlike those above). You do them because there's somebody watching, and a quarter-mile in 62 seconds looks a lot better than one in 89. Or you do them because "the guys will never believe that I got thirty-four miles today."

These errors — in fact, almost all of the mistakes that distance runners make — stem from a single source, the most common and most often ignored problem of self-coached runners: their tenacity.

Tenacity is the distance runner's stock-in-trade: if he didn't have it, he simply could not be a distance runner. Tenacity is what drives him on to finish the race when he wants to quit, what makes him pick up

---

*"3 × a mile" means running a mile at a certain pace (unspecified here), jogging a quarter-mile recovery (also at an unspecified pace here), and repeating the procedure twice. "16 × 220" means running sixteen 220-yard intervals with a given recovery between each. Similar notation is used throughout this book.

the pace when he's about to be passed, what makes him go out in the cold rain for the long training run he knows he needs.

But it can also be one of his most dangerous enemies, and this is especially true for the self-coached runner. In order to coach yourself successfully, you will have to learn to control your tenacity by injecting the note of reason into your workouts, by quelling your competitive spirit in training, by making sure that your body does not dictate to your mind. If you fail to do this, your inherent competitiveness will spoil your chances of competing at the top of your form.

Even the elite athlete is not immune to this malady if he is self-coached — as the example of Ron Clarke shows. Clarke's main attributes were his strong will and great physical strength, which enabled him to attack his training with the same ruthlessness he showed his rivals in racing. He frequently had world-class performances on the training track. I often speculate how Ron would have fared had he been coached in those years by someone who recognized that he had a serious problem with misdirected energy release in much of his training, and who could have redirected that release into major competitive efforts.

The endurance runner's competitiveness, his "killer instinct," is his strongest asset — in a race. If it begins to dominate training sessions, however, it can be just as deadly, and it will turn on the closest victim — the runner himself.

Developing a Training Schedule

The best way to overcome the common mistakes a self-coached runner makes in training is to develop a well-thought-out, feasible series of workouts that point toward a specific racing goal. With such a schedule a runner's tenacity becomes an asset even in training, as it helps him maintain his pace in the workouts and his attendance on the track.

SET YOUR GOALS

The first step is to set your goals. Begin by picking the distance you want to race. Since the training is different for each distance, you need to make one race your priority and focus on it. (As you train, you will find that your times for all distances will show improvement, but your races at the distance specifically chosen will naturally improve the most.) If you want to qualify for Boston with a marathon under 2 hours 50 minutes (2:50), you may want to make that your main priority. If your company has an annual 10K, and you want to crush the guy who always beats you at handball, pick the 10K. If you feel that your best distance is around 10 miles, you may want to train for that distance.

Once you've picked your distance, make sure that you have time enough to prepare for the race. You will need a weekly mileage base before you begin the training schedule (the amount of mileage base depends upon the race distance and the time you want to run: longer races and faster paces require more miles per week). You should run this base for at least four weeks before you are ready for the eight-to-ten-week schedule leading up to your race. In all, you need at least three months' preparation for your best performance.

SET YOUR SCHEDULE

After you have set your goals, set your schedule. Look over the schedules in Chapter 7 and find the one that best fits your capabilities. If you are not sure of your level, run time trials at the distances indicated: these will give you an accurate gauge of your ability. Thus, if you can run a 220 in 30 seconds, a 440 in 64 seconds, and a mile in 4:50, you are capable of running a 10K in 34:00 — after you've done the training.

You may wish to modify the schedule to fit the time you have available — for instance, moving the long run to Wednesday instead of Sunday, if that's more convenient for you. You can also make some changes in the workouts themselves as long as you preserve the balance between speed, strength, endurance, and stamina suggested for that particular schedule. See the next chapter for a full discussion of these elements of training.

WRITE IT DOWN

Once you have decided upon your schedule, write it down. This is especially important if you have altered the schedule, because it will help ensure that all the training elements you need are included. Even if you haven't changed a thing, it is a good idea to take a sheet of paper and put your schedule on it. The act of writing will commit you much more than a mental intention ever could. Then put it up on the wall where you can see it. If you haven't established a regular training calendar, now is a good time to start; you can write each workout in when you have finished it and compare your performance to the schedule. On the days when you know you should work out, but just don't feel like it (even a distance runner's tenacity weakens at times), the posted schedule and the calendar will help keep you going. A written workout calendar will also help you to reproduce your results in future races. If you see that a year ago you ran 16×440 in 82 seconds, and this year you can hit the same workout in 78 seconds (in the context of the same basic type of training), you know you should be able to race a little faster than you did last year.

GET SOMEONE ELSE TO LOOK IT OVER

After you have written out your schedule, get someone else to look it over. Since, as a self-coached athlete, you do not have access to a "real" coach, it is vital that you have someone to talk to about your training. Ideally this person should have an extensive knowledge of biomechanics, various physiological theories, massage, and injury treatment. The person need not be a runner, but he or she should be able to psych you up when you need it and calm you down when you're too pumped up. Although for the best results the person ought to be dedicated enough to learn something about running, just having someone to listen will often be enough for you to straighten out your own thinking. In fact, we all need someone like that, whether we're athletes or not.

You and Your Running Buddies

Most of us find that other runners fill this need best, and two or three runners can often help one another to improve far more than each would have been able to individually. Often a lot of good information on training will be exchanged on the weekly long runs, interspersed with jokes, comments on life, and recollections of past races.

These talks on the long runs or around the water fountains also have a drawback: the information isn't *always* good. You may hear that one of your competitors is running 140 miles a week, or doing 40×220 in 27 seconds. You may hear that calf's liver, or bee pollen, or spinach on whole wheat bread is all you need to improve your times 30 percent. You might as well hear that if you put a used insole under your pillow, you'll get a pair of shoes from the Tooth Fairy.

In 1982, when Rod Dixon was on a very successful tour of American road races, I asked him how many miles he was doing a week. He looked all around and — since we were alone on an elevator — said, "Al, I'll tell you: I do about seventy a week, no more. But I have to tell everybody over here that I do a hundred to a hundred and twenty. They expect it of a serious runner. And they just won't believe me when I tell them the truth."

The best way to get someone to look over your schedule is to offer to do the same for him or her. Expect to be challenged on certain workouts or goals. If you can't justify them, it's possible you made a mistake. Even very experienced athletes sometimes write down a workout they *hope* they can do, because it might give them a lift. But if they can't do it, they not only get down because they failed, but they have also lost a beneficial workout they could have done on the track that day. It's much better to find these workouts when they're still on paper.

At the same time that your buddies are evaluating your schedule, you should be looking over theirs. In this role you act as "coach," and you need above all to be the voice of reason. If one of your group has proposed a workout you think is beyond his capabilities, you're not doing him any favors by letting him try it without questioning. If he's been running 45-minute 10Ks, and he announces that this month he's going to break 37 minutes, ask him — politely — why he thinks so. On the other hand, if he seems capable of harder work, and you believe that it would help him, say so, and be prepared to give him your reasons.

It can also be helpful for you and your friends to train together at times, especially on the track and during the long endurance runs. Both track and endurance training require concentration and effort, and they seem easier with others around. There are, however, some important things to watch out for:

- *First,* don't do anyone else's workout.
- *Second,* don't try to impress anyone with your workout.
- *Third,* run the times on your schedule, or no more than 2 to 4 seconds off per lap. (See the guidelines, Chapter 7.)
- *Fourth,* don't compete in a workout. If you "win," you have won nothing; but if you lose, you will feel like a loser.

When you're not running with your buddies on the track, keep an eye on them when they're doing an interval. Check them from the side, back, and front, and compare their form with the section on ideal running form in Chapter 3. It is almost impossible at first to feel where your arms and legs are going; only a viewer can tell, and that's one of the reasons why the best runners are the ones who had coaches. Do not try to insist that one of your group change overnight from a shuffler to a sprinter, and don't try to do it yourself, either — just learn to be aware of how you're moving. More than anything else, a change in running form will be caused by the increased amount of track work you're now doing. The body adapts to become more efficient at the faster pace, and in doing so prepares to race more efficiently, too.

One good method to check track form is to use a camera — an instant-developing kind is the best, because you can see what you looked like while the "muscle memory" of what it *felt* like is still fresh. A video cassette recorder is even better, of course, since it allows you to slow down your running action for easier analysis.

There's one interesting sidelight to the use of cameras or videotapes. Each runner invariably feels that *he* has the worst-looking running form of the group. The reason for this is simple: you are accustomed to seeing your buddies run; in fact, you can probably identify them at a distance long before you can see their faces, just from their characteristic actions. Because of this familiarity, you have become used to the stylistic anomalies of your running partners, while they, of course, become used to yours. That means that the only one of your training group who can see your form with a fresh eye is *you yourself*; so be especially attentive to your own image — even though you will feel like flinching at the sight, if you're like most runners.

Consistency

One of the most valuable assets the self-coached runner can have is consistency. In training, consistency means the ability to do solid (not brilliant) track workouts, regular endurance runs, and reasonable mileage week after week, month after month, and year after year.

Unless you train with a knowledgeable coach, you may think (or instinctively feel) that your running can be improved much faster than it really can. You may pat yourself on the back for your foresight in doing six weeks of hill work before a hilly cross-country meet, or five weeks of track work before a 1500-meter race, but in fact the introduction of such work so short a time before the race may have as many negative effects as positive ones. (It takes at least a year, for example, for the body to "get comfortable" with the transition from road to track training.)

The belief in "instant solutions" is even more prevalent among runners training for distance events. How often have you heard a runner say, "Well, I've only been averaging about fifty miles a week for the last six months, but to get ready for the marathon I did two seventy-five-mile weeks and then two weeks in the nineties." If you were to ask him just before the race how many miles he'd been getting in training, he'd probably average his last six weeks and give you a figure in the mid-70's. But he probably won't race like a runner who has been doing 75 a week. Instead, he'll race like a 50-mile-a-week runner who has killed his legs in the month before the marathon — and that's exactly what he *has* done.

The same problem, with perhaps more serious consequences, seems to strike runners who are "coming back" from an injury or illness. They are often a little contemptuous of the mileage and the workouts they can comfortably and safely run, especially when they think about what they could do just a short while before. So they progressively increase the intensity, quality, and duration of their workouts, trying to get back to their previous level too fast. As a result, they burn out or break down before they return to full training. And while recovering from *this* setback, they frequently repeat the cycle.

Many runners think that the greatest enemy of consistency is a day off. Miss a day, they think, and that makes it easier to miss the next, and so on. As far as it goes, their reasoning is true; an occasional day off, while it can be a good idea, is also a taste of the lotus that can lead to too many days off.

But, given the generally compulsive nature of endurance runners, a day off isn't the threat to consistency that runners fear it is. A much more serious threat lies in excessive compulsion itself. How many training days have you lost in the last year to injury, burnout, fatigue, and other products of compulsive training? And how many to laziness?

Another serious threat to consistency lies entirely outside the world of running, in that other part of your life in which you have a job, a family, and a place to eat and sleep. A few world-class runners have cut this other world down to the minimum so that it doesn't interfere with their training. Bill Rodgers's often-quoted remark is, "No one who works a forty-hour week is ever going to beat me." Most runners, however, prefer to keep running only a part of their lives — although an important part. Sooner or later something unexpected is going to disrupt your schedule. When that happens, accept it in good part; remember that the runners used for the schedules in Chapter 7 often had similar disruptions but were nevertheless successful; and DON'T try to combine in one day a missed workout with the next one. The chances of injury are too great.

You can minimize the chances of losing a day's training by running as soon as you wake up — before anyone else is awake, before the office can call, before a problem with your house or car has been discovered. Then, when you get back home, whatever happens, you've got your workout in.

Running early is also a solution to the problem of maintaining consistency when your daily schedule is changed or disrupted. Many runners are surprised to find that their mileage goes *down* when they're on vacation, even though they should have more time available then to run. Because they don't have to get running early so they'll have time to meet some other commitment, they put it off until later in the day, and frequently end up canceling it entirely.

In summary, the key to consistency is dedication. But it's hard to be dedicated to a workout you're not sure you need, one you just thought up on the spur of the moment, or one you read about in a magazine. To overcome this problem you need an underlying philosophy of training.

TWO

The Philosophy and Practice of Training

IN FORTY YEARS OF RUNNING I have encountered many "prophets" who claimed to have discovered the perfect training method. Often a new prophet's approach is adopted by elite athletes of every continent — until another prophet replaces the "perfect training method" with one that is more perfect. But while the development of a new and innovative technique may lower the times of the super-elite, it always leaves behind a mass of runners who are convinced that they can't run with the hotshots until the prophet releases his secrets to the world. The main drawback of this evolutionary process is that, at any given moment, most of the world's runners are waiting to hear the most recent break-through, and consequently not concentrating on their running.

I came to the conclusion many years ago that there is no "magic formula." While there are many different training roads to success in distance running, all good training philosophies must be based on sound physiological principles and controlled by common sense. Then, if the runner works steadily and consistently, improvement is sure to follow.

Of course, a runner can modify a training program and incorporate new ideas as they prove themselves. Generally speaking, however, it is better to stick with a commonsense approach until one has accumulated enough experience to conduct some judicious training experiments. The best most of us can hope for is steady improvement and the realization that no training will magically turn a 7-minute miler into an Olympic champion.

Nor do you have to be born into a special environment, or train in one, to improve your running. In my time I have witnessed the development of world-champion runners in widely diverse regions of the world: the sandhills of Portsea, Australia; the mountain ranges of New Zealand; the Rift Valley and the high plateaus of Africa; the sunburned plains of Kansas; and most recently the streets of Boston and the trails of Oregon.

Method, not environment, is the key.

What Method?

We can judge a method most easily by seeing whether it produces the effect we want. Most distance runners want one effect above all: improved performance. My training philosophy is simple, but it has produced improved performances on two continents and in three decades of international competition.

Forty years ago, when I was first introduced to the sport of endurance running as a thirteen-year-old, training knowledge was almost nonexistent. Runners trained twice a week and raced on weekends, and athletes under twenty were discouraged from training and racing for fear of burnout. Women distance runners simply did not exist. It was in this wasteland of distance-training information that I began to learn the art of running and slowly started to synthesize the concepts that have been successful for me and for most runners who have diligently applied them to their own training.

The method I use is based on the concept that every aspiring runner — old or young, male or female, fast or slow — has four inherent capacities: speed, anaerobic capacity, endurance, and stamina. Although inherent, these capacities are not fixed; they can be developed and honed by specific training, and the result will be improvement at all running distances.

• *Speed* is the ability to run quickly over short distances — 200 meters or less — where oxygen debt is not a significant factor. (Oxygen debt occurs when oxygen cannot be transported rapidly enough by the blood to supply immediate energy requirements.) Speed depends on inherent capability more than any other of the four capacities, but every runner can run faster by learning how to use what inherent speed she or he possesses.

• *Anaerobic capacity* is the ability to withstand oxygen debt. Physiologically, the human capacity to perform without sufficient oxygen is very limited, but we can, with proper training, develop greater anaerobic capacity. Anaerobic capacity is usually the limiting factor in distances longer than a sprint but less than a mile.

• *Endurance (aerobic capacity)* is the ability to run a distance greater than a mile while maintaining a substantially elevated heart rate — near maximum — *without* incurring a debilitating oxygen debt.

• *Stamina* I define as the ability to run long distances at a submaximal heart rate — for example, 10 to 30 miles at a slow pace.

While it is obvious that some race distances require more of one capacity than of the others (for a dash, you need speed; for an ultramarathon, stamina), it is important to realize that to race well at any distance between one and 50 miles all *four* of these capabilities must be developed.

A runner, if he or she chooses, may develop each capacity in a training session devoted to it alone. For example, a *speed* workout might consist of very fast 110's with a long recovery. An *anaerobic* workout might be moderately fast 110's with a short recovery. An *endurance* workout is usually several miles at a fast yet comfortable pace. *Stamina* is traditionally developed by long, slow distance running.

It is frequently more efficient, however, to develop two or more of these capacities in a single workout, as the schedules in Chapter 7 demonstrate. You may see 2 × 2 miles at a brisk pace (short endurance) sandwiched between two sets of 4 × 110 yards fast (speed), while a long 20-mile weekend run (stamina) may include 6 to 12 miles at a faster pace (long endurance). Similarly, speed workouts can spin off from anaerobic training. (But while increased ability to handle anaerobic, aerobic, and stamina training will automatically result in greater speed, the opposite effect does *not* occur. That is, increased speed will not improve the operation of any of the other three components, even though it will, of course, improve your race times.)

Endurance versus Stamina

Since both endurance and stamina are usually developed in long training runs, many runners (and many coaches) fail to distinguish between them. Failure to make this distinction, however, can lead to serious training errors.

In *endurance* running, the limiting factor is always the body's ability to supply itself with and efficiently use oxygen. When the body cannot supply enough oxygen to the working muscles, only a few minutes of anaerobic capacity remain before the runner must slow. If you try to maintain your pace, acute physiological distress occurs. Your legs may not be tired, but you will feel generally rotten all over.

Runs to build *stamina,* however, should never find you limited by your aerobic capacity because your heart rate should reach only 130–150 beats per minute — substantially below the 170+ level that may be reached in an endurance effort.* What usually limits, and finally stops, a runner in a long stamina run is tiredness in the muscles of the legs.

Most runners know the difference between anaerobic fatigue and "dead legs," but too many ignore the difference in their training. Suppose you read that Craig Virgin runs a 21-miler once a week at a 6:30 pace. The next Sunday you discover that although it's tough, you can do it too — in fact, you can do it several weeks in a row. Now the only difference between you and Virgin is his track work, right?

Wrong. Virgin's 21-miler is at a pace so slow for him that it's all stamina; his cardiovascular system is having an easy workout as he runs. For you, the run is long endurance; your heart rate is way up as you try to hold the pace. Such an effort may give you a psychological lift, but it will almost surely affect the rest of your training: you won't be able to hit the speed, anaerobic, and short endurance work as hard. If you repeat your 21-miler for a number of weeks, you'll definitely develop your long-endurance capacity (if you don't burn out first). But you probably won't race very well, even in the longer races that demand good endurance capacity, because you'll be undertrained in three of the four areas that determine how well you race.

*It is traditional that your maximum heart rate (beats per minute) should be "220 minus your age," and a good training rate should be around 150. But these rates vary widely in the running population, and should not necessarily be taken as gospel. The best guide is to run the times and the paces indicated in the schedules; your body's response will be automatic.

Aerobic/Endurance versus Anaerobic Training

The border between aerobic and anaerobic training is just as clear-cut as that between stamina and endurance, and just as important. It is the rate of work at which the body first becomes unable to supply its muscles with sufficient oxygen. This limit varies from runner to runner, and it is important to determine where your own line is because some of the most valuable training consists of flirting with oxygen debt. As you run the workouts in the schedules in Chapter 7, you will gradually develop the ability to sense the point at which your body approaches this zone.

Ability to race fast is primarily dependent not on one's best short distance speed but on the ability to *hold* a slightly slower speed. Each of us is born with a certain amount of innate speed. Nothing we can do will change it. Instead, to improve our racing, we strive to sustain whatever speed we possess over longer distances and longer time periods. As the preceding section on stamina and endurance indicated, the key to developing this ability is the heart.

Emil Zatopek, the famous Czech distance runner, got the jump on the rest of the world in the late 1940's when he reasoned that since the heart was a muscle, it could be strengthened. Accordingly, Zatopek developed a training program that stressed the heart, then allowed it to recover slightly, then stressed it again. This was the birth of interval running, and this type of training (work-recover-work) is the foundation of all modern training methods. Zatopek's breakthrough enabled him to win the distance runners' Triple Crown in the 1952 Helsinki Olympics (5000 meters, 10,000 meters, and marathon). Even though runners have since made many refinements in Zatopek's methods and have surpassed all his best times, no one has managed to equal this great feat.

Interval training is often misused by runners who fail to realize that it is training primarily for the heart. For example, let's say that you are training to run a sub–34:00 10K, and one of the workouts on your schedule calls for 16 × 440 yards at 85 seconds, with a 220-yard recovery jog between each effort. Since an 85-second quarter is a 5:40-mile pace, you might think, "This workout is too easy — I can run four miles straight at 5:40's. Why break it up with unneeded 220 jogs?"

The answer lies, of course, in the way the heart is exercised. If you were hooked up to a heart monitor during the workout, you could see that your heart rate accelerates and then stabilizes in each 85-second quarter that you run. When you start each 220 jog, your heart rate begins to drop. At the end of each recovery, your legs accelerate you quickly to your 85-second pace, but your heart rate lags slightly behind, perhaps not reachng a stable higher rate until halfway through the quarter. Thus, as you alternate running and jogging, your heart is intermittently subjected to slight anaerobic pressure and forced to catch up. This does not occur in a 4-mile run at a 5:40 pace because there the heart establishes an efficient rate and maintains it for the duration of the endurance effort.

On the other hand, some runners look at an interval workout of slow quarters as an excuse to "hit it" — for them, quarters on the schedule at 85 seconds are more likely to be run in 72. Here the heart gets hard work and the legs get even more, and the resulting tiredness will carry over to the week's other training (some of which is going to be directed toward the leg muscles, which were scheduled to have an easy day running 85's).

The idea that interval work is "supposed" to be a killer is probably the most common misunderstanding of Zatopek's breakthrough. One of my runners once looked over the first schedule I made for her and said, "But, Al — I can do *all* these workouts." That is, of course, the idea. It would be a lot easier to coach runners if all I had to do was to give them workouts they couldn't do.

As you can see from the above examples, it is often not the "hard" workouts that are the hardest to do. Most runners get "psyched up" for a really tough workout, while a lot of slow intervals can seem tedious and boring. Often it takes self-restraint in training to run times which are slower than your ability. This aspect of interval training has its place in coming up, too: the discipline and tenacity you develop in these workouts will pay dividends in your races.

Speed Work

Speed is a two-edged sword: there are probably as many good runners who hurt their ability to race by overdoing speed training as there are good runners who get beaten by someone else's superior speed.

On the other hand, you can't afford to ignore speed work, as a little simple math will show you. The average runner has about 50 percent "fast-twitch" muscle fibers — the genetically determined component of muscle tissue which governs your basic speed. Obviously, it would be an error to neglect such a large potential source of running energy. But let's assume, for the sake of argument, that you are one of the very rare runners who has 99 percent slow-twitch fibers. Surely you can afford to ignore speed work then? No. If developing that 1 percent of fast-twitch fibers means a 1 percent improvement in your pace, consider that 1 percent of a 3-hour marathon pace is more than 4 seconds per mile. Or to put it more graphically, a loss of 1 percent from your performance costs you 17.6 yards per mile, at *any* pace, fast or slow.

A runner who finds that he has less than average speed may think he needs *more* speed work than the naturally gifted. But if you make that "logical" assumption, you will find the end result disastrous: biology dictates that the *slower* your inherent speed, the *less* speed work your body can tolerate. Long, slow distance (LSD) training has countless devotees today because of runners who made this mistake, burned out, and concluded that speed work didn't help them.

Because of this, and the inherent chance of injury in all speed workouts, you should be cautious in the number of workouts you do rather than risk all your training for one extra workout. The guidelines in the schedules in Chapter 7 generally restrict speed work to once every two weeks. Furthermore, these guidelines are for active training that is directed toward an upcoming race. When peak-level performances are not required for a month or two, it is wise to cut the number of speed workouts to reduce both the chances of injury and the increased psychological pressure speed work brings with it. Similarly, during the winter months when the cold weather makes muscles tight and injury-prone, your training should be adjusted toward more endurance and stamina work, and away from speed.

SPEED THROUGH THE BACK DOOR

Doing speed training once every two weeks may not seem very often, especially when you consider that serious sprinters may do three hard speed workouts in one week. Fortunately, there is a "back door" to speed training that allows you to get a lot of the benefit without the danger.

Middle-pack runners can use this technique by running two to four fast but relaxed "pickups" of from 60 to 110 yards after their warmup or at the conclusion of a workout. More serious runners who train twice a day can introduce a series of four to ten strides (from 60 to 150 yards) at a fast, relaxed pace into their morning runs four or five days a week. These strides should feel easy — that's how you escape the problem of burnout — but you can look back over a month and see that you have shoehorned the equivalent of an extra four or five speed-work days into your regular schedule.

Introducing speed through the back door leads to a progressive buildup without teardown, and, more important, allows the runner to work on the technique of sprinting and the smooth conversion of distance-running form into sprinting form. As you become stronger and more confident with speed training, additional refinements may be added, including acceleration: stride normally for the first half of your pickup, then sharply increase your rhythm and hold it for the second half. Do not try for "speed at any cost"; concentrate on holding sprinting form and quick turnover (fast rhythm, not long strides). When all these components are integrated and are consistently practiced, a distance runner can develop awesome finishing ability.

The career of one of my runners, Len Hilton, serves as a good example. Although Len didn't have much inherent speed, he worked hard for several years to master the technique of explosive acceleration. It paid off for him when he ran against Marty Liquori (who was also a famous kicker) in the 1973 U.S. mile championship. At the 1500-meter mark in the race, Len was in fourth place, fifteen yards behind the leader, Liquori. Len's explosive acceleration brought him to the finish line fifteen yards in front. He had gained thirty yards in the space of 120, against one of the best kickers in the history of the mile. Len's time for the 119.6 yards between the 1500-meter mark and the mile finish was an astounding 13.9 seconds. For many years this clocking stood as the fastest finishing split in sports history. Len's attention to the technique of explosive acceleration was rewarded by two national championships and the honor of representing the United States at 5000 meters in the 1972 Munich Olympic games.

The Track

A lot of runners hate the track. Many of them are the ones who were burned out by interval-happy coaches in high school or college, or those who burned themselves out by hitting every track workout as hard as they could. These runners justify their aversion by pointing out that many of the top distance runners rarely do track work, preferring roads, trails, or hills.

Unless you are as experienced in assessing running effort as the top distance runners are, you need the discipline and structure of track workouts twice a week. (If you, like many runners, associate the track with intense speed work, you may sense a contradiction with the earlier statement that speed work should be less frequent. There is no contradiction, though; as you can see from the schedules in Chapter 7, the track serves as an ideal site for anaerobic and endurance training as well as for speed.)

Track training has several benefits:

- An accurately measured course (if your favorite road or trail mile is off by only 1 percent, your times will be off by several seconds).
- Safety (no cars, fewer muggers).
- A reliable way to measure progress.
- An easier way to provide training structure.

The most common objection to track training is that it is boring. It can be, but it does not need to be. A runner can introduce a number of variations in traditional interval workouts that will produce helpful *psychological* results in addition to the physiological benefits.

A good example of this is the "ladder" workout: a session of progressively increasing or decreasing distances — for example, 110 yards, 220 yards, 440 yards, 660 yards, and beyond. A runner may work up the ladder (a "step-up"), running progressively longer distances, or down the ladder (a "step-down"). Going up, the runner learns that running similar speeds for increasing distances produces less physical discomfort than he feared. On the other hand, speeds can be increased progressively as the runner moves down the ladder, and this can lead to a significant psychological boost and a "training high."

The bottom line of track training is improvement. At the worst, you will come to feel for the track the same grudging admiration you may now have for some rigorous teacher you once hated in school.

Training for the Marathon

Over the years that I have been associated with endurance running I have seen many changes, but none so spectacular as the love affair with the marathon that started in America in the late 1970's and spread throughout the world in the next five years.

Time after time I have seen an individual begin running (for whatever reason), then begin tentative forays in competition — usually the 10K "fun run" variety. Then, at some point in the runner's career comes the dramatic announcement: "I want to run a marathon."

Sports psychologists have given little attention to why people subject their bodies to the physical rigors and mental stress of this event, except to say that it's a "fad" and that those who compete are following a "herd instinct."

I do not believe that the marathon is a fad or that it will soon lose its popularity. The reasons we run marathons are rooted in the question of why we run in the first place. The first book I ever read on running was Dean Cromwell's *Championship Technique in Track and Field*. The University of Southern California head track coach and former U.S. Olympic coach implied in the introduction to his work that running was a survival trait that had been blunted by centuries of civilization. Cromwell was a practical coach and went no further than this observation.

Many years after Dean Cromwell's death, William Glassner, a practicing psychiatrist, wrote a best-selling book called *Reality Therapy*. Glassner identified and refined the insight Cromwell originally had about running. Glassner, I understand, is not a runner, but used running as a practical tool in psychotherapy. He coined the term "positive addiction" to describe the condition that runners invariably develop after commitment to a long-term and consistent running program. Running, theorized Glassner, becomes a "positive addiction" because we have evolved from those who had to run to stay alive, and this survival mechanism is genetically programmed into our physiological and psychological makeup. Hence running makes us feel good, physically and mentally.

While I think that the survival connection with running is logical and persuasive, it still does not answer the question, "Why the marathon?" instead of some other long distance.

Most endurance runners know the story of the purported beginning of marathon running. We will never know for certain whether there ever was a Greek warrior named Pheidippides who ran from the plains of Marathon to Athens to carry the news that the Greeks had defeated the invading Persian army, and dropped dead in the agora as soon as he had gasped out his message.

It does not matter whether Pheidippides existed or not: the important thing is that his legend has survived, and legends persist in cultures because they satisfy some cultural need or objectify some basic truth. (After all, no one knows whether Oedipus was "real" or not.)

So the legend of Pheidippides persists, a runner who ran so far so fast that he died. And it is undeniable, unfortunately, that runners have died while preparing for, running, or recovering from a marathon. While the risk is small for the average competitor, I have no doubt that some of the marathon's attraction comes from flirting with the danger of death.

Subconsciously, that risk is probably present in the minds of all marathon runners. Look at the vocabulary they use: at 22 miles (Pheidippides' distance) they "hit the wall"; they even joke that Pheidippides was the first to do so. A lead pack is typically "killed off" by the pace until only one — the winner — survives. Finally, consider the most commonly heard excuse at the post-race dinner: "I went out too fast, and died."

The connection of the marathon experience with death is visceral as well as mythic and verbal. There is probably no other experience in your life which will leave you feeling as close to death as a marathon that goes wrong. Ask a runner what it feels like to "hit the wall." (Never mind whether sports physiologists have been able to reconstruct the mechanism; a marathon runner will know exactly what you mean.) The images he will use will be those of terminal illness; the symptoms (nausea, dizziness, weakness, breathlessness, depression, and pain) are the worst the body can suffer. Many real deaths are probably easier.

Then there's the other side of the coin. Physically, survivors of the marathon are promised better health and longer life. A few doctors make the claims explicit: complete a marathon, and you will never die from a heart attack.

The psychological rewards are less tangible, but no less real. The "traditional" American hero is a frontiersman, whether Miles Standish or John Wayne. But Americans no longer possess frontiers to test themselves against. (The single most common statement I hear from native-born Americans when they discover I'm originally from Australia is that my homeland is the "last of the great frontiers.") Now, instead of a long trek in a covered wagon during which a man and a woman can face uncertainty and risk, Americans have created their own last great frontier with the marathon, and a significant and growing part of the population is attempting to repeat history in a unique way.

It is because of all these physical and psychological factors that the marathon is frequently compared to childbirth. How many other sports events can make that claim? Both are intensely physical and profoundly emotional experiences that can produce cathartic responses after the event — crying jags, euphoria, and not infrequently post-partum and post-race depression. Both childbearing and marathon running share one more similarity, as I see it: both produce their emotional involvement not only because of their physical effort, but because each successful childbirth, each successful marathon, is a triumph for life.

RUNNING UNDER THREE HOURS

The 3-hour marathon is the mid-range runner's 4-minute mile; for him there is no barrier as exciting or challenging. Many athletes spend years of frustration attempting to achieve this goal, only to come away empty-handed — not because they did not have the ability, but because they lacked the knowledge to coach themselves to their goal. If you can run a mile in 5:35 and a 10K in 38:30, you can train yourself to run a marathon in under three hours.

Two of my runners who had completely different backgrounds illustrate how planning and proper training can result in a sub–3:00 race. Both possessed the desire and determination and had satisfied the mile and 10K time criteria. Diane, a twenty-six-year-old student and part-time teacher, had been running for four and a half years. Her fastest marathon was 3 hours 14 minutes. Glenn, a forty-nine-year-old banking executive who had run for three years, had a best marathon of 3 hours 11 minutes. Diane had exceeded the mile and 10K time standards by a margin greater than Glenn's, and had faster inherent speed. Their schedules were modified slightly to reflect these differences.

The planning for their attempts to run under three hours began six months before the actual races took place. Both decided to aim for races on December 4, 1982: Glenn would run the Tucson Marathon in Arizona while Diane selected the Dallas White Rock Marathon. In July 1982 both runners began a concentrated twenty-week training program. They both had to contend not only with Houston's heat and high humidity but with the other problems — nagging injury, soreness — that occasionally affect all endurance athletes. The schedules below indicate where these problems occurred and how each individual dealt with them.

Both runners had competed during the spring racing season. In the early summer, Glenn took a three-week vacation, working out lightly but consistently, while Diane ran competitively on the track to develop her speed.

In July and August, each runner averaged 65 miles a week. A typical week's training consisted of:

- one long stamina run of 12 to 18 miles at 7:30 to 8:30 per mile
- two track workouts that included one of the following:
  - 16 × 220 yards in 38 to 40 seconds each, with a 220- to 440-yard recovery in between
  - 12 × 440 yards in 85 seconds each, with a 440-yard recovery in between
  - 5 × 880 yards in 3 minutes each, with an 800-yard recovery in between
  - 3 × 1 mile in 6 minutes to 6 minutes 10 seconds each, with an 880-yard recovery in between
- four days of easy running (6 to 10 miles) at 7:30 to 8:30 per mile.

We planned for both Diane and Glenn to run the New York City Marathon six weeks before their target races as part of their preparation. They were both to run about thirty seconds per mile slower than the 3-hour pace, and so would finish in 3 hours 13 minutes. However, they both had the option of running New York faster if conditions were good and they were further along in their conditioning than we had anticipated.

3–Hour Marathon

Here are their schedules beginning September 27, 1982 — ten weeks before their major efforts at Dallas and Tucson:

All track workouts in both Diane's and Glenn's schedules (and in every schedule throughout this book) are preceded by a warmup and completed with a warmdown.

"Easy running" in both schedules is 7:30 to 8:30 per mile.

Diane	Glenn

1st Week ("Day 1" is a Sunday)

Day

	Diane		Glenn
1	16 × 220 in 38 — 220 R*	1	12 × 220 in 38 — 330 R
2	10 miles in 70:00	2	5 miles in 32:30
3	2 × 1 mile in 6:00 — 880 R	3	4 × 880 in 2:53 — 880 R
4	10 miles in 70:00	4	6 miles easy running
5	6 miles easy running	5	6 miles easy running
6	½-marathon in 1:23:15	6	10K race in 39:57
7	18 miles easy running	7	24 miles easy running

2nd Week

Day

	Diane		Glenn
1	5 × 660 in 2:15 — 660 R	1	7 miles easy running
2	10 miles easy running incorporating 5 miles in 32:30	2	2 miles in 12:45, 1 mile in 6:15, 880 in 3:05 — all 660 R
3	4 × 1 mile in 6:00 — 660 R	3	7 miles easy running
4	Rest day	4	3 × 1 mile in 6:20 — 880 R
5	5 miles easy running	5	12 miles easy running
6	5 miles easy running	6	Ill — no running
7	20K race in 1:16:23	7	Ill — no running

*Run 220 yards in 38 seconds, 16 times, with a 220-yard recovery in between.

Diane	Glenn

3rd Week

Day

1. 15 miles easy running
2. 12 × 220 in 43 — 220 R
3. 10 miles in 70:00
4. 10 × 440 in 90 — 220 R
5. 6 miles easy running
6. 12 miles in 84:00
7. 15 miles easy running

4th Week

Day

1. 10 miles easy running
2. 2 × 1 mile in 5:45 — 880 R
3. Rest day
4. 2 miles in 12:00 — 880 R;
   4 × 220 in 40 — 220 R
5. Rest day
6. 5 miles easy running
7. 3 miles easy running

5th Week

Day

1. New York City Marathon — did not finish
2. Rest day
3. 1 mile easy running
4. 3 miles easy running
5. Recovery — no running
6. Recovery — no running
7. 11 miles easy running

6th Week

Day

1. 2 × 880 in 3:15, 2 × 440 in 86, 2 × 220 in 39 — all 440 R
2. 10 miles easy running
3. 12 miles easy running incorporating 6 miles in 42:00

3rd Week

Day

1. Ill — no running
2. 3 miles easy running (New York)
3. 7 miles easy running (New York)
4. 12 miles easy running (New York)
5. 10 miles easy running (New York)
6. 7 miles easy running (New York)
7. 15 miles in 1:45:00

4th Week

Day

1. 6 miles easy running
2. 4 × 880 in 3:15 — 440 R
3. 6 miles easy running
4. 2 miles in 12:40

5. 6 miles easy running
6. 4 miles easy running
7. 4 miles easy running

5th Week

Day

1. New York City Marathon 3 hours 10 minutes 13 seconds
2. 5 miles easy running
3. Recovery — no running
4. Recovery — no running
5. Recovery — no running
6. 6 miles easy running
7. 6 miles easy running

6th Week*

Day

1. 9 miles easy running

2. 5 miles easy running
3. 11 miles easy running

*Week's training affected by injury.

Diane	**Glenn**

6th Week (cont.)
Day

4 12 × 440 in 88 — 220 R
5 13 miles easy running
6 7 miles easy running
7 20 miles easy running

7th Week
Day

1 13 miles easy running
2 3 × 880 in 2:55, 3 × 440 in 84, 3 × 220 in 40 — all 330 R

3 A.M. 15 miles easy running
   P.M. 10 miles in 70:00
4 2 × ¾ mile in 4:30, 880 in 2:52, 440 in 80 — all 330 R
5 13 miles easy running
6 5 miles easy running
7 25K race in 1:38:18

8th Week
Day

1 15 miles easy running
2 10 × 220 in 39 — 220 R
3 A.M. 18 miles easy running
   P.M. 7 miles easy running
4 6 × 880 in 2:52 — 660 R
5 12 miles easy running
6 6 miles easy running
7 21 miles in 2:20:00

9th Week
Day

1 15 miles easy running
2 2 × 440 in 80, 330 in 57, 4 × 220 in 39 — all 220 R
3 13 miles easy running
4 6 miles easy running
5 13 miles easy running
   incorporating 5 miles in 31:00
6 10 miles easy running
7 15 miles easy running

6th Week (cont.)
Day

4 8 × 440 in 88 — 220 R
5 10 miles easy running
6 9 miles easy running
7 8 miles easy running
   incorporating 6 miles in 41:00

7th Week*
Day

1 12 miles easy running
2 3 × ¾ mile in 4:45, 3 × 880 in 3:10, 3 × 440 in 95, 3 × 220 in 45 — all 440 R
3 15 miles in 1:41:00

4 12 miles easy running

5 6 miles easy running
6 6 miles easy running
7 25K race in 1:45:13

8th Week
Day

1 12 miles easy running
2 10 × 220 in 45 — 440 R
3 10 miles easy running

4 5 × 880 in 2:55 — 660 R
5 12 miles easy running
6 5 miles easy running
7 15 miles in 1:40:00

9th Week
Day

1 15 miles easy running
2 8 × 440 in 90 — 440 R

3 10 miles in 71:00
4 12 × 220 in 42 — 440 R
5 15 miles in 1:42:30

6 12 miles easy running
7 9 miles in 57:00

*Week's training affected by injury.

Diane	Glenn
10th Week	*10th Week*
Day	*Day*
1 8 miles easy running	1 12 miles easy running
2 8 × 440 in 85 — 220 R	2 2 × 440 in 95, 2 × 1 mile in 6:05 — all 660 R
3 Rest day	3 Rest day
4 5 miles easy running	4 2 miles in 13:00
5 Rest day	5 Rest day
6 3 miles easy running	6 3 miles easy running
7 Dallas White Rock Marathon December 4, 1982 2 hours 52 minutes 58 seconds	7 Phoenix Marathon December 4, 1982 2 hours 57 minutes 24 seconds

It is interesting to note that both runners encountered serious physical problems during the course of their training and yet were able to achieve their goals in spite of them. In Glenn's case, a bout of illness in the second and third weeks forced him to restrict his training; nevertheless, he was able to finish New York faster than his schedule called for. A serious muscle pull in his groin hampered him in the sixth and seventh weeks, finally clearing up only twenty days before the Tucson marathon. Yet he was able to achieve his goal.

The lesson to be learned from Glenn's experience is that schedules are not carved in stone. When injury forces you to change them, you may do so without ruining your chances of meeting your goal. Unfortunately, many runners in Glenn's shoes would have tried to "push through the pain" and ignore the injury, and would have succeeded only in being unable to race.

The New York City Marathon was a disaster for Diane and clearly illustrates a different point: the inherent risks of marathoning even for the experienced runner who has a coach. Although the weather in New York was windy and cool, it seemed reasonable to expect good running times. Diane, however, experienced nausea and dizziness early in the race and was forced to stop after eighteen miles. After waiting for thirty minutes in the cold, she felt a little better and began running again. Her symptoms returned, and a Houston orthopedic surgeon saw her weaving and urged her to drop out.

Diane followed his advice and made it to one of the numerous first-aid tents before collapsing with uncontrollable shaking. Her temperature was 90°F. She was rushed to a local hospital where intravenous fluids were administered and emergency measures were initiated to elevate her body temperature and control her violent shaking episodes. Although her recovery was relatively swift, she had to be carefully monitored by electrocardiogram as her temperature began to rise.

Diane's condition was diagnosed as "chronic dehydration." This problem should never have been allowed to develop. Diane had mentioned to me one day in training that she was cutting out most of her diet drinks; she felt she was consuming too many of them. I should have immediately cautioned her to *replace* her depleted fluids with water or some other suitable commercial preparation. Add one more humbling experience for this coach, and a reinforced awareness of something I should never forget: "The price of trauma-free endurance running is eternal vigilance."

Al Lawrence, early in his career, lost his form and nearly lost this race.

THREE

Form

FOR SELF-COACHED RUNNERS, one of the most elusive aspects of good running is correct form. Even if they are aware of its importance, many runners find it difficult, without a coach, to decide exactly what constitutes good form and even harder to determine how close they are to attaining it.

Often, self-coached endurance runners assume that correct biomechanical movements are important only in highly technical events — the sprints, the hurdles, the jumps, and the throws. But when you consider that there are about seven thousand foot strikes and arm swings in a 10,000-meter race, the importance of mechanical efficiency becomes obvious.

While all athletes have slight to significant variations in the way they run, there are general running techniques that will help you improve your form. Incorporating into your own running style basic mechanical principles shared by all champions can result in greater efficiency, easier movement, and increased relaxation — all of which add up to faster races.

Fundamentals of Good Running Form

As you read the following description of techniques for improving your form, remember that good form cannot be obtained overnight, nor is it absolutely necessary for good running. Watch national-class athletes, and you will see that even they have flaws. (In fact, watching other runners of any level is a good way to learn to analyze form, and with practice the lessons you learn watching can be applied to your own running.)

HEAD

Hold your head up naturally; it should be aligned with your trunk, not tilted to one side, forward or back. Avoid tensing your neck or facial muscles. Focus your eyes several yards ahead of you, whether you are on a trail, cross-country course, track, or road. Occasionally glance at the horizon to give yourself a sense of spatial perspective. The direction of your eyes is important because, generally speaking, where the eyes go, the head follows, and the head should be held steady to ensure body balance. Avoid a stiff, robotlike effect; a minimum of side-to-side movement of the head is acceptable, but it shouldn't throw you off balance even slightly.

You may see a runner in a stressful finish throwing his head back, but this is a serious error: it tightens the neck muscles and causes the trunk to bend back, thus shortening the stride and slowing the runner just when he needs an extra burst of speed. (In the late 1950's, Soviet runners were taught to prevent this error by keeping the tip of the tongue resting against the base of the lower front teeth, right at the gum line, as they ran. They claimed that it was impossible to commit a serious head-form error as long as the tongue was in that position. If you tend to throw your head back, you might try their solution.)

BREATHING

Breathe freely through your nose and mouth. Your breathing should be as natural as possible, given the conditions imposed by your effort. "Breathe deep" from the diaphragm so that you are using all your lung capacity; your stomach should move out as you breathe in. This will also help prevent a stitch.

UPPER BODY

Your torso should be almost upright, with just a suggestion of forward lean. This is the Australian "up-runner" posture. The chest should be consciously lifted to free the action of the diaphragm. (Think of the typical male behavior when he meets a female at the beach.)

During the finishing sprint of a race and during speed work, the forward lean grows more pronounced. This is the body's natural reaction to the increased drive of the legs. You can easily see this in a sprint race — watch the tremendous forward lean of the sprinters as they accelerate out of the blocks. When they approach top speed, their rate of acceleration slows, the degree of forward lean is reduced, and their bodies approach the perpendicular.

The shoulder and arm on each side of the body should move in concert with the opposite leg: that is, the right shoulder and arm move forward as the left leg moves forward, and the left shoulder and arm move with the right leg. Keep your shoulders relaxed, not hunched up. They should move only slightly; a small rolling action of the shoulders is the body's normal response to the turning of the hips during the stride.

In endurance running (as opposed to sprinting), your arms should move smoothly: the upper arms forward and back from the shoulder; the lower arms slightly across the body, never crossing the centerline of the torso. The arms should be used primarily for balance and for counteracting the torsion created by the action of the legs.

In sprinting, the arms move powerfully forward and back and seldom cross the body. The power of the leg drive in sprinting is influenced by and is proportional to the power and thrust of the upper arms.

Your hands should be carried closed, but not clenched. Clenching the hands leads to premature fatigue in the forearms, upper arms, shoulders, and neck.

Hold your thumbs close to your loosely clenched fists, with your wrists rotated so that your thumbs are on top and thus roughly parallel to the ground. Your thumbs will point approximately in the direction you are running, except for a slight movement toward the centerline of your body at the forwardmost point of your arm swing. Holding your thumbs properly helps prevent forearm tension and the inefficiency of loose or floppy wrists.

Your elbows should be bent at approximately 90 degrees, but this angle increases as your arms swing past the front of your body and decreases as they swing past your hip on their way back. In other words, your elbow is not locked, and your forearm stays roughly parallel to the ground throughout the arm's range of motion. Not only is unlocking the elbow more efficient in producing energy transfer, but moving the arm muscles through a range is less tiring, too.

THE LEGS

While there are three distinct phases involved in a single stride from beginning to completion, it is the smooth, uninterrupted flow of movement integrating these phases that creates a seemingly effortless running action, and you should try to keep that in mind. We'll describe the three phases in turn here for clarity: the *plant*, or support, phase; the *driving* phase; and the *recovery*.

The *plant* seems to cause runners the most difficulty. Initially, the athlete's first contact with the running surface is with the *outer* edge of the foot, with the knee slightly bent (don't worry about making sure you do this; almost everyone does it right without even thinking). At slower speeds, your foot will probably touch at the outside of the heel first; as your speed increases, the point of impact will move forward, toward the ball. Your foot then rolls inward (pronation), so that the entire sole (including your heel) meets the ground. At this point your knee is supporting the weight of your body, and your body's center of gravity should be directly over your foot.

Beginning runners who have heard this advice often have trouble with its implementation; frequently they lean forward to bring their torsos over the foot strike, but succeed only in throwing themselves off balance and running inefficiently. The body is usually pretty good at making the necessary adjustments on its own, but you can help it along by thinking of moving your *hips* forward and over the landing leg while keeping your upper body erect. This not only keeps the center of gravity over the point of contact, but makes the following drive or leg thrust smoother and less tiring.

The *driving* phase begins when the foot on the ground pushes against the running surface and propels the body forward and up. The leg straightens, and the foot rolls forward onto the toe and makes its final push.

The *recovery* phase begins as the driving leg breaks contact with the ground. The leg flexes at the hip, knee, and ankle as it tucks up toward the buttocks. The movement can be thought of as an aircraft retracting its landing gear.

For part of the recovery phase, the runner's body is not in contact with the ground. Then the opposite foot lands and the entire process begins again. The runner has completed a single running stride. The goal, of course, is to repeat this sequence as smoothly and efficiently as possible for the thousands of times necessary in every distance race.

Errors in Running Form

There are several common problems that can prevent you from achieving a smooth, efficient running stride. You have probably seen them in a lot of your fellow runners, and even in some of the best runners in the world. Nearly everyone deviates in some way from the norm.

But the fact that Emil Zatopek always looked as if he were having a heart attack, grimacing and clawing at his chest as he set world records, or that Alberto Salazar leans too far forward and dips slightly to one side, doesn't help *you* run any better (although it does show that bad form won't keep you from being a champion — if you're good enough). It takes a lot of practice before you get good at knowing where your arms and legs are during each phase of the running action. As we've indicated in the first chapter, it is a good idea to have a fellow runner check out your form. You can also use the videotape or snapshot approach, or watch your shadow, or catch your reflection in store windows as you run by.

The most common errors that you will see in your fellow runners — and perhaps in yourself — are these:

• *Awkwardness* is hard to define, but easy for you to recognize in other runners (and in videotapes of yourself). It is also frequently easy to cure. Often it is merely a matter of "too few miles" — not on a weekly basis, but total miles run in your career. During the first two thousand miles or so, most awkwardness gets smoothed out, and the runner is left with a workable, if not perfectly smooth, style.

• *Problems in arm carriage* tend toward two extremes: either you point your forearms toward the ground, dissipating energy you could save with correct forearm drive, or you carry your forearms high in front of your chest, losing power and tiring yourself out by hunching your shoulders. Both these problems can be corrected if you remember to (1) alternately touch your hipbones with the heels of your hands, then your elbows, and (2) keep your forearms parallel to the ground.

• *Loose or floppy hands* cause loss of power in the stride. You can see this for yourself if you try to pump your arms hard and let your hands flap at the same time. Most noticeable in sprinting action, this error costs almost as much in endurance running without being so noticeable. The best solution is to remember to hold your hands so that your thumbs are on top. Your wrist has a limited action when held this way, so that even if you still have a tendency to flap your hands, you can't.

• *The shuffle,* as its name implies, means running with very little leg lift and very short strides. Usually the result of training exclusively with long, slow distance runs, the shuffle isn't a problem if you're going to run an ultra-marathon: it is an extremely efficient form of running for a long distance. Because it conserves energy so well, though, it is not a good way to run fast — any pace under 7:30 per mile is about the limit. Any tendency you have to shuffle will be cured, by and large, by running on the track as you follow the schedules in Chapter 7. The faster running automatically refines your style slowly, over a period of weeks and months.

• *Overstriding* is the opposite of the shuffle. In an effort to run faster, the runner reaches out with his foot an extra inch or so, and in so doing moves the foot plant ahead of the body's center of gravity. When this happens, the first job of the leg muscles is to "catch" the runner as he comes over the lead foot, and so the muscles use energy to *de*celerate the runner before they accelerate him again. The proper way to increase stride length is by thrusting more vigorously with the rear leg during the driving phase. Even when one increases stride length in the most efficient way, however, this extended running action is nearly always more tiring and less efficient, and extracts more from the runner than the increased speed warrants.

• *Asymmetrical running action* — a marked difference in form between the two sides of the runner's body — can be either structural or merely habitual. Habitual asymmetry can be overcome — after someone has pointed it out to you, since most runners who have it aren't aware of it — by consciously working to keep your action symmetrical and within the limits of good form as outlined above. *Structural* asymmetry is frequently caused by one leg being shorter than the other (although that can be mimicked by running day after day on a slanted road). Structural asymmetry, if it needs correcting, has to be checked by a doctor. An asymmetrical running style, however, will not necessarily prevent you from running well. Bill Rodgers's asymmetrical form (his left arm pumps back and forth as it should, while his right arm moves in a circle as if he were stirring cake batter) is reportedly caused by a discrepancy in leg lengths.

Mental Form

Many running books that concentrate on running form fail to mention its most important aspect — the mental attitude of the runner. Mental form is not what your high school P.E. teacher meant by "When the going gets tough, the tough get going." That addresses the problem of tenacity; and while tenacity is an important element in the development of good competitive endurance runners, there is a state of mind that enables the endurance runner to perform far more efficiently than mere tenacity ever can.

To describe this state of mind, we'll borrow a concept from the Romantic poets, and call it "rapt intransitive attention." Briefly stated, you have achieved this state when your body is relaxed as you run, and your mind is alert and "turned inward."

Rapt intransitive attention may seem like a very complicated concept, but it is not that difficult to master if you work on it in your training.

The first step is to practice running with an awareness of your body's motions. Gradually move your mental focus up your body, starting with your feet and progressing toward your head. Check your action against the description of good running form which opened this chapter. This drill is especially fruitful during long endurance runs, when your body is repeating a close-to-racing action at nearly race pace mile after mile.

Check your form consistently until it becomes an ingrained habit; then you will check it unconsciously but no less frequently. One of the best techniques for developing relaxation is to concentrate on the upper body. Most tension in runners comes from the upper body, logically enough, because the lower body, doing most of the running, doesn't have the leisure to get tense.

Upper-body tension seems to hit runners in two stages. The first stage, usually confined to novice runners, involves tightening the fists and, for some reason, tensing the tongue. The solution to these problems is often simple awareness: that is, as soon as the runner becomes aware of this tendency, he can begin to overcome it. And (because of the association of this type of tension with novice runners) the problem seems to cure itself, like the other novice form errors, after two or three thousand miles.

The second stage of upper-body tension is much more widespread among runners, and much more difficult to get rid of, because the two or three thousand miles that were eliminating the earlier problems seem to intensify these: hunching the shoulders and knitting the brows. Both of these problems rob your body of energy that it needs to run; neither contributes anything to your pace or your endurance; and worst of all, both problems lead to localized pain that affects your ability to monitor your body's functioning as it runs.

The stylistic "mnemonics" to use to help yourself overcome these problems have been mentioned earlier. For tense shoulders, concentrate on trying to touch your hipbones with your elbows as you swing your arms during your running stride (this drill has the advantage of improving your arm drive, too). For your forehead, concentrate on placing your tongue at the base of the lower front teeth. Combine these routines with a *conscious* effort to relax. If you find that you don't remember to relax often enough, you may want to train yourself, for example, to think "Relax" every fourth stride, or every time your watch turns over a new minute, or whenever or however best suits you.

The ability to run with concentration and relaxation at the same time — to control energy as you release the power of your body — is the final result of rapt intransitive attention. A runner who can achieve this state will be able to improve his endurance running greatly.

In fact, a lot of runners slowly move toward and discover rapt intransitive attention without knowing it. You have seen them yourself — their faces relaxed and void of expression, their eyes focused, apparently, on something not visible to ordinary mortals. It is this image of distance runners, in fact, that seems to provoke the most criticism from nonrunners: "Why don't they smile? They look like a bunch of expressionless zombies."

According to several elite runners, however, rapt intransitive attention is not the end of the road to ideal mental form. Many great athletes report the sense of temporary dissociation from their bodies during hard races — the feeling that they were somewhere "up above" watching themselves run, and thus were able to make objective judgments about pace, stride length, and so on. Many found that that sense of dissociation was combined with a feeling of weightlessness and effortlessness, as they ran easily into the lead and on to the finish line, feeling as if they could run forever.

For most of us, this stage will remain merely theoretical, and we will have to be content with relaxation and controlled release of energy. But, if you race enough and not too much, there will be a race or two in your career in which you will glimpse something like the elite runner's dissociation, and you will be able to run faster than you have ever run over a given distance, and it will feel easy.

When it happens, remember as much of it as you can, because you will run that race in your mind's eye for the rest of your life.

Dr. Herbert L. Fred, ultra-marathoner, cools off during a hot race.

FOUR

Injuries, Stress, and Burnout

ATHLETES, ESPECIALLY SELF-COACHED ATHLETES, never seem to worry about injuries until they get injured. In fact, you are most injury-prone during that "golden zone" you may enter in the weeks before a big race, when you are strong from your training but don't yet have the pre-race jitters. This is the time you feel bulletproof; it is also the time when you are most likely to do something stupid.

You need to worry about injuries, or at least think about them, when you're well and injury-free. Practicing *preventive sports medicine* is one of the things a good coach would do for you, but it is possible to do it for yourself. After all, no one knows your body better than you do (even if you don't always act like it).

Preventive Sports Medicine

The two golden rules of injury prevention are the standard ones in endurance running: "know thyself" and "listen to your body." As is usually the case, the simplest rules are the hardest to follow; it takes years to develop fully your ability to follow these rules. Fortunately, there is more specific advice: to minimize the risk of injury, watch the "five S's" — shoes, stretching, surfaces, schedules, and stress.

SHOES

Your feet hit the ground about eleven hundred times a mile, cushioned only by about half an inch of rubber. When you look at it that way, it's amazing that runners are injured as little as they are. The main key to staying injury-free is to make sure that you wear the right shoes for the kind of running that you do.

The three criteria to look for in running shoes are cushioning, stability, and weight. Lack of cushioning (as in ultra-light racing flats and most spikes) transmits impact shock up the legs, increasing the chance of injury to the bones and joints. Lack of stability (often found in thick, cushiony shoes) allows the foot to roll to one side or the other. Such instability can lead to pain and injury of the tendons, ligaments, and muscles of the leg, especially in or around the ankle or the knee. Heavy shoes (frequently recommended for jogging) can be a factor in soft-tissue injury, such as a muscle pull, when you try to run hard in them.

Since about 1977, shoe companies have made great improvements in reaching the compromises that produce good shoes for endurance runners. Compromises are necessary because of the material used in running shoes. Cushioning is available by adding thickness, but this causes additional weight and a loss of stability. Stability can be gained by using stiffer rubber, with less cushioning and more weight. Light shoes are easy to build — just leave out the cushioning and the stability — but once around the track in them is all your legs can stand.

The shoe companies have done a good job of resolving those problems in the runner's favor. Almost all of the major manufacturers make shoes that combine lightness with stability and cushioning to a degree never before achieved. There are two drawbacks to this situation, however: high-technology solutions are expensive, and the price of running shoes has escalated even faster than they have improved. Even worse, now you can't blame a bad race on your shoes anymore. In your worst race this year, you wore better shoes than Frank Shorter wore when he won the 1972 Munich marathon.

When you shop for running shoes, go to a store that sells several different brands, because some seem designed for wide feet, some for narrow feet, and some for average feet. At the store, be wary of a salesman who wants to sell you a particular brand or shoe before he finds out what type of running you do. It's usually a good idea to find out what kind of running the *salesman* does, and evaluate his ability to give you good advice. If he is a sprinter, he might be very helpful if you're buying a pair of spikes, but less informed about shoes for ultra-marathon training, and vice versa. (If he doesn't run at all, be careful.)

One mistake that self-coached runners often make is checking the shoes worn by the best runners in the area, assuming that runners who are fast know all about the best shoes. That assumption has a grain of truth in it: most elite runners do high-mileage weeks, so they know what shoes hold up under that training. But in general, this is not a good way to shop; a top runner might have a different type of foot from yours, so what is comfortable for her might not be good for you at all. There is also the likelihood that you'll be seeing her most often in races, where she'll be wearing racing flats, not training shoes. Frequently the top local and national runners are given shoes by the shoe companies, and once they're getting free shoes, they usually just wear what they are sent instead of spending their time (and their money) finding the best ones.

In general, try to get a shoe with support, cushioning, and a fairly light weight. You will probably have to accept a little extra weight to get the other two qualities, but in most cases, the heaviest (and most expensive) shoes in a manufacturer's line are not the best for the kind of training you're going to be doing as you follow the schedules. For most of your running, a *training flat* offers the best combination of support and cushioning; this is the type of shoe you will want to wear in your slow recovery days, especially. If you are going to race in *racing flats,* be aware that because they are lighter (and therefore somewhat faster), they have less cushioning and less support and thus make you more susceptible to injury. Some runners do all their workouts in training flats and put racing flats on just for races, hoping to minimize the chances of injury by cutting down on the amount of time spent in racers. This is not a very effective way to train, however; not only do you need to do some workouts in the shoes you will race in so your body can adjust to the more efficient action of racing flats, but training exclusively in heavy shoes and then putting on very light ones for a hard effort is a good way to get injured.

That is even more true of spikes. Many runners, aware of the reputation spikes have for causing injury, try to avoid them entirely in training, and put them on only to race. By doing so, however, they deny the body time to accustom itself to the tremendous forces generated by running in spikes, and so predispose themselves to injury *during* the race. Even if they escape injury, they usually lose a week or ten days of training following the race because of soreness and stiffness. It is an old rule of running that you train in conditions similar to those you will experience in the race, so if you will be racing in spikes in your 5000- or 10,000-meter race on the track, be sure to spend a little time each week in spikes. As a rule of thumb, start off with no more than a mile of spike wear (including speed and jogging) and build up to no more than three or four miles a week. For example, bring your spikes to one track workout a week, warm up (and warm down) in training flats, but wear your spikes for the fast work in the middle of the workout. For the other track workout that week leave your spikes at home.

STRETCHING

Stretching is a controversial topic. Some runners swear by it, claiming that if they don't stretch they are sure to get injured; others like Marty Liquori call it "overrated," while Gordon Pirie scoffs that you never see racehorses stretching before a race. Adding to the confusion is the fact that studies have shown a positive correlation between stretching and running injury — that is, those runners who stretch are *more* likely to get injured than those who do not. This does not mean, however, that stretching *leads* to injury: runners who discovered that they were prone to injury might have developed a regular stretching program in an effort to ward it off. In any case, too much stretching may make you sore and may interfere with your running for several days. Furthermore, you should always resist the urge to "stretch out" an injury, since this can make it worse.

All in all, however, gentle, moderate stretching of the muscle groups that running tends to shorten (calves, hamstrings, lower back) is probably a good idea. (See Chapter 7 and the section on the warmup for specific exercises.) Additionally, side leg lifts from a reclining position seem to be a good strengthening and stretching exercise for the adductor and abductor muscles of the thighs, when running makes them sore and stiff.

SURFACES

Where you run has a lot to do with your chances of becoming injured. The trade-offs in your choice of surfaces are similar to those in shoes — more cushioning means less stability and so on.

• *Grass* and *tanbark* tie for the softest surfaces a runner can enjoy. (Tanbark is the gray-brown fibrous material often used on jogging trails.)

Both offer nice cushioning without too much loss of stability. Both are good for slow, gentle jogging and not quite so good for long endurance runs (the soft surface increases the effort required to hold a given pace and so effectively increases the stress of the workout). The main problem is the occasional hole, sometimes concealed by long grass.

• *Asphalt* is frequently used in older roads. It is more stable and "faster" than grass or tanbark, and softer than concrete, but it too has drawbacks. Some of them are obvious: roads have cars on them, so be careful, especially at night; they also have potholes. A less obvious drawback of many asphalt roads is their pronounced "crown" — high in the middle, sloping steeply toward the sides. If you constantly run on such roads, run in the middle whenever possible, and alternate sides if you can't stay in the middle. If you always run on one side, the leg on the high side (toward the middle of the street) tends to overpronate, and the increased strain may injure that leg. Even if you avoid that problem, you face another: constant running on a slope creates a muscular imbalance in your legs, with the "uphill" leg strengthened from dealing with the foot's pronation. Significant muscle imbalance nearly always leads to injury to the weaker muscle, in this case the thigh muscle of the curbside leg.

• To some extent, this advice also applies to *concrete* roads, although they usually have less crown than asphalt roads. The main injury hazard from concrete is that it is one of the hardest substances that your feet will ever hit. Some runners just can't tolerate the constant jarring, and must train on softer surfaces. Unfortunately, many races are run on concrete, and you should do at least some training on the surface you'll be racing on, both to have a better sense of pace and to feel a little more "at home" during the race. Obviously very stable, concrete seems "fast," but the constant jarring it gives the legs actually causes them to tire more quickly, making runs over about five miles more difficult than they would be on asphalt, for instance.

Track surfaces can vary almost as much as road and trail surfaces, and like them, each has its particular strengths and weaknesses.

• *Dirt* tracks are soft, but dusty in dry weather and boggy when it rains. Most runners will use a dirt track only when there is nothing else available.

• *Cinder* tracks are usually made of crushed brick, not cinders; if they have been well maintained, they can be excellent tracks. Usually they are softer than the new synthetic surfaces and less likely to cause injury (although you may not be able to feel the softness as you run). They can, however, become dusty if not maintained; the surface can get a little loose, so your feet slip; and they get hot and hold their heat, so that your feet may blister in a long workout on a hot day.

• *Asphalt* is usually the next step up, frequently built when a school is converting from cinder but doesn't have enough money for a fancy polymer surface. Asphalt tracks are usually easy to identify because they're black. They are very hot, but that seems to be their only drawback — the surface is springy, with good traction, wet or dry.

• *Synthetic* tracks are the state of the art in running surfaces. Recognizable by their bright colors and composed of what looks like chopped-up rubber bands cemented together, they are the fastest tracks you can find. They are also slightly cooler than asphalt or cinder. They do have some drawbacks, though: a minor one is that they get very slippery in a light rain, so that you need spikes for interval work. A more serious problem is that the speed built into the track comes from the rebound effect of the rubber surface — it is designed to "spring" the runner forward as he toes off. But because these tracks are built for fast high school and college runners, the rebound effect is designed to work at paces faster than five minutes a mile. Slower runners will not get a "spring"; they'll get a jar like a secondary foot strike. Thus synthetic tracks may increase shock-related injuries among slower runners (and among fast runners when they jog). Perhaps the greatest problem with these tracks is that they are very expensive and tend to wear out quickly; many track coaches will not open their synthetic tracks to the public. If you do find a synthetic track to run on, don't abuse the privilege: keep to the outside lanes while jogging your recovery laps and use the inside lanes (which wear out first) only when you're running a timed interval.

Because of the track's reputation as a breeding ground for injuries, some runners make a point of reversing directions every few laps in order to "unwind" a little. They feel that doing so minimizes the risk of injury caused by running the curves and stressing the body asymmetrically. There is probably nothing wrong with doing this for the jogged recovery laps, but the hard intervals should *not* be run clockwise (unless an injury forces you to) because interval training in the same direction as track races toughens the mind and the body for the stresses of track competition. (Besides, running a fast interval against the usual flow of track traffic is dangerous.) If you are worried about track-related injury caused by the curves, it makes more sense to run your intervals in one of the outside lanes, where the stresses around the curves are greatly reduced.

SCHEDULES

One of the easiest ways to get injured is to arrange your schedule so that you do twice your usual amount of one particular type of work — speed, anaerobic training, aerobic endurance, or stamina. Nearly all running-related injuries are "overuse" injuries: that is, they are caused by using the same muscles, tendons, bones, and joints over and over. Obviously, it is hard to avoid this in running.

By rotating your work among the four categories, however, you can reduce the cumulative stress. Speed tends to use and develop the quadriceps (the muscles along the fronts of the thighs), while slower running develops the opposing muscles (the hamstrings) along the backs of the thighs. Speed and fast anaerobic work develop the big muscle at the top of the calf (the gastrocnemius), while slower paces work the soleus (the long flat muscle in the lower calf). Both ends of the speed spectrum (very fast and very slow) seem to develop skeletal muscles, while anaerobic and endurance work stress primarily the heart and lungs.

The schedules in Chapter 7 stress different areas of the runner's body in a given week, so that the chances of injury through overuse are greatly reduced (but not completely eliminated).

STRESS AND BURNOUT

Both physiological and psychological stress can predispose the body to injury. This is especially true of the syndrome commonly called "staleness," "flatness," or "burnout."

Burnout is characterized by tiredness, lack of "spring" in the legs, frequently an elevated resting heart rate, and insomnia or waking up in the middle of the night. Other symptoms vary from runner to runner. Like having the blues, everyone burns out a little differently. A true medical illness such as mononucleosis or anemia may masquerade as burnout, but fortunately this happens rarely.

Burnout usually hits novice runners for the first time when they are starting to build their mileage. Everything usually goes along fine, the miles pile up, and then *wham*! You may have a cold that comes back as soon as you try to increase your mileage again. Or you may feel apathetic — you don't care whether you do your daily run or not.

The best treatment is simply to jog easily until you feel like running hard again. Don't try to force yourself, because that will only push you farther into the burnout tunnel and delay your return to normal. Furthermore, because your body's defenses are weaker now, any hard running will only expose you to the danger of other types of injury.

Sometimes, however, this malady seems to be self-perpetuating — the longer you jog easily, the *less* you care about running a hard workout. Usually the cure in this case is to force yourself to do a speed workout. The fast work seems to pop you out of the flatness, and you will feel like resuming your regular training. This remedy is tricky, however, because hitting the speed work too soon will flatten you out again. Be especially sure that you are *physically* over your flatness; you should probably wait a week after you *think* you should be feeling better before you try the speed-work cure.

To prevent burnout, keep a close watch on the amount of stress in your life, both running-related and non–running-related. The stress of thinking about a job change or of moving may be just as hard on you as the kind you can quantify on your running calendar. Even your regular mileage can be extra tough if you do it in extremes of weather, unfamiliar surroundings, high altitudes, or dirty or polluted air.

One problem about stress from non–running-related situations is that it is almost impossible to evaluate numerically. It's easy to see that a hard 21-miler is stressful, and roughly how it compares to a 10-mile jog, but it's much more difficult to tell whether having your boss over for dinner is harder than having a toothache for a week, and how both compare to an all-out 10K in the heat. Be conservative.

What to Do When Injury Hits

In spite of your precautions, sooner or later you will probably get an injury. When you do, *stop running immediately.* Don't complete the workout or the race.

If you've never been injured, you may think that that is the silliest advice you've ever gotten from a coach. But if you've ever suffered a running injury, you know how easy it can be at the time to ignore it. Occasionally, you may not even know you're hurt until after the run. (One runner in the 1982 Boston Marathon made the national news by running a time in the mid–2:40's, in spite of the fact that his femur had snapped at the 5-mile mark. Except for brief transitory pain when it broke, he perceived no difficulty in running until he collapsed in the finishing chute when he tried to walk.)

Here are some telltale signs to help you distinguish between a transitory "glitch" and a real injury:

- Intense incapacitating pain (this one is easy).
- A feeling that something structural has altered.
- Pain that increases progressively.
- A feeling like a needle or an insect sting in a muscle.

If you're *not certain* whether you're hurt or not, stop running and walk or jog until you are sure one way or the other. No workout is worth an injury. If you're in a race, and suspect you're injured but can't tell for sure, ask yourself how important the race is. If it's merely part of your buildup for a more important race, drop out if you can, jog in if you must. If it's *the* race, run it until you know for sure. But then, if you decide you are injured, get out immediately — and preserve your chances of running again.

First aid for running injuries traditionally involves the mnemonic ICE: ice, compression, elevation. Besides being easy to remember, the initials also occur in order of relative importance.

Ice is applied to the injury after being wrapped in a towel. Do not place the ice directly on the skin. Apply it for about 10 minutes, take it off for 10 minutes, then reapply it for 10 minutes. This alternation should continue until ice has been applied for at least 30 minutes. This procedure can be repeated four to six times in 24 hours.

Compression reduces swelling in the area of the injury. It can be combined with ice therapy by wrapping the ice pack fairly tightly over the injury with an elastic bandage. When the ice pack is removed, the elastic bandage should be reapplied so that compression is maintained.

Elevation, while not always possible, is another way to reduce swelling in the area of the injury.

Another important treatment of a running injury is to take a pain reliever. Of these, *aspirin* is the cheapest and most widely available. It is also quite effective. Not only does aspirin help relieve the pain of the injury, but it also reduces the inflammation in the injury site. Other pain relievers do not necessarily have this capability. (If aspirin upsets your stomach, buffered varieties are available.)

At this point you have done as much as you can for your injury, as far as first aid is concerned. There are still two treatments you can administer to help your injury heal itself.

• About 48 hours after the injury, you can begin to use *heat* on the injury site to increase circulation and reduce muscle spasm. You may use a heating pad, a hot water bottle (with a towel), a hot tub, a whirlpool, or whatever similar heat source you have available — but the heat shouldn't go above about 108°, nor should it be applied for more than about 30 minutes at a time.

• If you have an injury to "soft tissue" — muscle pull, muscle tear, muscle spasm (they all feel about the same) — you *should* try to jog within the limits of pain. Doing so may speed the repair process and make it more complete, leaving a minimal scar in the muscle tissue. Failure to exercise the injured muscle can result in a palpable lump of scar tissue at the site after the injury has healed.

RUNNING-RELATED PROBLEMS

There are a few injuries the self-coached runner needs to know about, either because they're so common and frequent, or — in the case of heat-related illness — so dangerous.

• *Black toenails* are often caused by shoes that are too short, but they may also be caused by shoes that are the right length but are too wide, allowing your foot to slide forward until your toes hit the end. Another cause (often overlooked) is that you may unconsciously raise your toes as you run, hitting the top of the toe box even when the shoe is the correct length for your foot. Be sure to buy shoes that are the right length and the right width, and that have a deep enough toe box.

• *Blisters* are caused by heat, usually from friction. You can decrease friction by applying petroleum jelly to your skin and by wearing additional socks (be sure that your shoes have enough room for extra socks, though, or you may trade blisters for black toenails). Don't run in the same pair of shoes every day. If you do get a blister, let the fluid out with a sterilized needle, pad the blister and surrounding skin, and watch carefully for infection.

• *Sciatica* is, correctly speaking, compression of the sciatic nerve. Most runners use the term to refer to aches and pains of the lower back, buttocks, and hamstrings. Occasionally these will be combined with pain or numbness in the lower leg and the foot. Because this problem is often caused by the overdevelopment of the muscles of the lower back, thighs, and buttocks, you can sometimes get relief by stretching these muscles regularly, and doing exercises to strengthen the abdominal muscles.

• *Heat-related illness* — especially heatstroke — can be lethal. Your knowledge of it not only can protect you yourself, but can help you look out for your fellow runners as well.

Heat-related illness occurs most frequently during races run in high temperatures and high humidity, although it can also occur during races run in "ideal" conditions. Similarly, the longer the race, the greater the chance that heat-related illness can hit, but runners have suffered from it in races as short as 8 kilometers (just under 5 miles). Often a mistake in pace judgment is the trigger that leads to collapse. Thus it usually strikes novice runners, but racing greats such as Alberto Salazar and Jim Peters have been hit by it, too. Two major errors that predispose runners to heat problems are (1) insufficient training for the race distance, and (2) an ill-advised attempt to pick up the pace too fast in the last stages of the race.

Common symptoms of heat-related illness (in approximate order of appearance and increasing seriousness) are:

• Muscle cramping.
• Nausea, vomiting.
• Headache, dizziness.
• Gooseflesh on the chest or upper arms.
• A break in running rhythm to a "drunken" gait.
• Confusion or disorientation.
• Incoherent or slurred speech.
• Collapse.

If you notice that your running is wobbly or if you feel confused, ask for help immediately. If you notice any of these symptoms in a fellow runner, get aid for the person as soon as possible.

Treatment consists of cooling and rehydration. Frequently these measures must be instituted very quickly to prevent permanent brain damage or death. Cooling can be done with wet towels and crushed ice. Sometimes the victim is immersed in a tub of ice water, as Salazar was when he collapsed from exertional heat illness at the Falmouth Road Race. Intravenous rehydration can be necessary in severe cases, although merely drinking cool water is a more usual treatment.

Prevention is usually a matter of paying attention to your training and your body's signals, and *regular hydration* — not just during the race, not just the day of the race, but for days before the race, whether you're thirsty or not. (And for *weeks* before the race if you're training in hot, humid weather.) Drinking a sufficient amount of fluids to keep your body hydrated should be a routine part of every runner's training.

• *The Stitch.* The person who finally figures out how to prevent the stitch will be unanimously voted the Nobel Prize for Sports Medicine. A stitch usually manifests itself as a sharp pain just under the right ribs. Aside from its characteristic location, it is typified by tenacity.

Stitches that occur in other places on the torso seem to be much easier to overcome. Those on the *left* side under the rib cage may result from too much food or water in the stomach; while painful, they are usually transitory (although sometimes a left-hand stitch will lead to a right-hand stitch a few minutes later). A stitchlike pain lower in the abdomen, below the waist, is frequently just gas, and may go away if you press on the painful area firmly. Heavy carbohydrate consumption and too little water seem to cause this problem especially.

The cause of the true stitch has been widely debated. It has been ascribed to stomach cramps, gallbladder irritation, duodenal gas, an engorged liver, and various other ailments of muscles and organs. The most likely source, however, is the diaphragm, because the stitch is clearly related to breathing.

To the extent that there is anything you can do about the stitch, it seems to respond best to being treated as a cramp or spasm of the muscles of the diaphragm. The most effective cure is to stop running, but of course that's not usually an acceptable solution. What works as well as anything else is to *breathe out against resistance* — purse your lips together while exhaling, for example. This may help the muscles "work out" the spasm, and if it is successful, this method will last as long as you remember to use it. Another frequently described cure is to bend forward and press on the location of the stitch. Usually this gives only temporary relief, and the stitch returns. Some runners report that they can cure their stitches by placing their right hands on top of their heads as they run.

Stitch prevention creates as much discussion as the causes and the cures. Bent-knee sit-ups to strengthen the stomach muscles are often recommended. They may help prevent stitches caused by bad posture and the usual swaybacked tendency that high mileage causes, but it is not clear that strengthening the muscles of the stomach wall will help strengthen the muscles of the diaphragm.

A few elite runners who suffer from the stitch have apparently arrived at other workable solutions. One world-class marathoner, for example, believes that he can control his tendency to stitch by taking antacids before he races; others say it's not the antacids themselves, but the simethicone in them (an agent that is supposed to help expel gas). If you suffer from stitches, these remedies are worth trying; at the worst, they'll be no less effective than the old runner's trick of crossing your fingers on the spot and saying a prayer (or swearing, according to your faith).

Joan Benoit's solution is even better. In the 1983 Boston Marathon she was far in the lead when she felt a stitch coming on at fifteen miles. So, she says, "I slowed the pace down . . . took some water, collected myself and moved on." She moved on well enough to set a world record of 2:22:43. So the next time you get a stitch, just slow down and collect yourself, and get back on pace. Simple, huh?

When You Need to See a Doctor

The best advice here is to see a doctor whenever your injury or complaint of whatever type doesn't seem to be getting any better, or, worse, when it regularly interferes with your training.

What kind of doctor should you see?

A few years ago, the choice was pretty limited: you went to a doctor who was a runner himself, if you could find one. Even if his specialty was neurology or obstetrics, he was likely to have had enough running experience, combined with his basic medical training, to help.

Now, after the running boom, the problem is just the opposite: there are so many specialists available to the runner that choosing the right one can sometimes be difficult. Obviously you should try to go to a doctor who treats a lot of runners. But you need to be more selective than that and pick the type of doctor you think you need. The more accurate your choice, the faster you can get treatment and get well. Here's a brief list of specialists.

Internists (not *interns*) are specialists in internal medicine. The right one, especially a good diagnostician, can be very helpful in treating the whole body as a running organism. Your feet, for instance, may hurt because you're overweight. Lose weight and your feet may stop hurting.

Some runners have exercise-induced asthma; others will have bloody urine after a long run. For problems like these you should consult an internist.

Orthopedic surgeons give surgical and nonsurgical care to bone, tendon, ligament, and muscle injuries. An orthopedist who deals with runners usually knows what works and what doesn't for running injuries. The treatment may be quite different from that for a similar injury sustained in a car wreck or football game.

Podiatrists are not medical doctors, but they *do* specialize in taking care of the feet. Again, podiatrists who work with runners tend to know more about running-related foot problems than the usual podiatrist. An internist or an orthopedic surgeon who diagnoses one of your injury problems as stemming from a foot or leg imbalance may send you to a podiatrist for treatment or for an orthosis — a plastic or rubber insert to be worn inside your running shoe, designed to compensate for some abnormality or imbalance in your running action.

Chiropractors specialize in the manipulation of the body to overcome imbalances, including those which occur during running. Because the profession of chiropractic is occasionally looked down on by physicians, it is sometimes a "last resort" for injured runners. But many runners feel that chiropractors have helped them, especially with lower-back problems and with sciatica (see "Running-related Problems").

When you look for a specialist, ask for recommendations from your family physician and from experienced runners who have had injuries. Doctors who run, whether or not they treat running injuries, usually know specialists who do. If you need a particular type of care and you go to the wrong specialist, he probably can refer you to the right one. If you feel, however, that your treatment isn't helping or your progress is unreasonably slow, don't hesitate to consult another specialist.

Recovering from Injury

After an injury, a runner has a lot of time to think. Usually he thinks about how dumb he was to do the workout that produced the injury, and he swears he'll never do it again.

He's making another mistake. Injuries usually aren't caused by one foolish workout, even though they may appear catastrophically in one.

They are the product of a long period of preparation in which the ground-work is laid: the chain of events that culminates in injury is the "dark side" of the weeks of training for an important race.

Just as each successful race is the logical outcome of two months or more of training, so each injury must be evaluated in its context. Nearly every potential injury "telegraphs" its approach; your best hope of avoiding the next one is to figure out what signals your body sent that you ignored.

While you're doing that, jog easily, especially if you have soft-tissue injuries. If you cannot run, take up some form of exercise that will not injure you further but that will keep your cardiovascular fitness close to the level it was. Most runners turn to stationary bicycling and swimming as alternatives. But if you also lose your cardiovascular fitness, be prepared for a long recovery period of several months before you return to the condition you were in before you were injured.

FIVE

Competition: Transcending the Limitations

FOR A SELF-COACHED RUNNER, the most difficult part of endurance training is the last week before competition. During the active phase of training, you are doing enough mileage with enough intensity to convince yourself that you are improving. Because of that, it is easier for you to employ common sense in your training and to maintain the consistency which keeps you aware that your running is steadily getting better.

Then, just when your training is going really well, the week before the race arrives, and the training process seems to stop. Many inexperienced runners (and a number of experienced runners, too) find this situation disorienting. They are on a training "roller coaster" and have no idea how to get off, or even that they should get off. They worry that if they ease up they will lose all the benefits of their pre-race training, or that they will feel sluggish during the race. Some are reluctant to give up the security of regular training experiences for the uncertainties of competition.

Competing is largely a *learned* skill, so it is not surprising that a lot of runners have these feelings. By concentrating on the psychological and physical techniques discussed in this chapter, you can train yourself to handle the final days before a major competition, and you may even learn to enjoy the "taper" as a rest period that has been earned and is richly deserved.

The Taper

The taper is the decrease in mileage and intensity of your running in the last five to seven days before major competition. The aim of the taper is to put a finishing touch on your running skills, to bring you to the starting line physically in excellent condition and psychologically honed to a competitive edge. If done correctly, the taper will let you approach your competition like a gladiator, but, unfortunately, major mistakes in the final days before a race can turn a potential gladiator into a noncompetitor.

To avoid the critical errors in tapering that most self-coached runners make, follow these three DON'Ts:

• DON'T try to force your training during the last five days to make up for what you feel are deficiencies. If you don't have the necessary training behind you, there is no chance that you can have a major breakthrough in the last five days.

• DON'T make the common mistake of trying to "sharpen up" with speed work during your taper. This is perhaps the single most common error that inexperienced endurance runners make. A last-minute speed workout will simply flatten you for several days and leave you with no "snap" in your legs for the race.

• DON'T try to maintain your normal weekly mileage during the last days before major competition. The super-elite may cover high mileages the last week before a race they are "training through," but for you to try to train through a major competitive race for which you've prepared for weeks is just bad sense.

To balance the DON'Ts, there are a number of DO's to work toward in your taper:

• DO begin a slow reduction in the intensity and quantity of your workouts before a *major* competition. This gradual easing up will allow your body to disperse the residual fatigue products that have been carried from one workout to another, so that your legs will have maximum snap in them on the day of the race.

• DO include one last quality workout not more than seven and not less than five days before major competition. This allows you to look back on a significant workout to gain a psychological lift during the days of enforced idleness at the end of the taper. (As the endurance runner becomes more seasoned and experienced, the last quality training session can be moved closer to the competition, but you should be conservative while learning your art.)

• DO take a day off before major races. Even those most set in their ways have found that changing their taper after many years has produced improved performances and a more relaxed approach to competition.

• DO concentrate on getting adequate rest and sleep on the days before competition. Most endurance runners don't. Even if you sleep well the night before the competition, you can't make up for sleep lost during the previous week. A very effective way of ensuring your rest is one that I hit upon twenty-five years ago in international competition, and it still serves me well. Before a major race on Saturday, I take Thursday as a complete rest day and then work out very lightly on Friday. This schedule has two benefits. First, using Friday as an "active rest day" takes care of apprehensions and minor worries, and the light exercise helps me sleep better. Second, remember that there is a two-day lag in the training effect — that is, a hard workout seems to affect you more the second day. Resting two days before the race turns that two-day lag into a valuable asset. You have time to feel the full benefits of your rest.

The Pre-Race Warmup

Many commonly heard comments after a race (often used to excuse a poor performance) are related to the warmup: "I mistimed my warmup," you may hear, or "I got to the race too late to warm up," or "I warmed up too much before the race started, so I was tired all the way through."

Although a lot of runners realize when they've messed up their pre-race warmup, many self-coached runners don't really know *what* they should do in a warmup, and *why*.

The purpose of the warmup is to prepare the runner for the upcoming race. Much of the preparation is directed toward the expected physiological stresses, but the warmup is also a useful tool to prepare psychologically for the approaching competition. As you improve as a competitor, the psychological preparation assumes greater importance.

To achieve these physiological and psychological goals, there are some general rules you should observe in your warmups:

• Use the same warmup routines before a race that you use for your track workouts (see page 90). By employing a consistent warmup routine before your track workouts, you will have removed most potential bugs before you try competition. Remember that before a race you should do no more stretching than you usually do before a track workout. Don't let nervousness lead you to overstretch. There is, however, one difference between workout and competition warmups: track workouts begin immediately after the warmup is completed, while the competition warmup should be timed to finish 15 to 20 minutes before the race starts.

• Take into consideration the prevailing weather conditions. If it is very warm, the warmup should be slightly shortened; if very cold, slightly lengthened.

• Get to the race well before the scheduled starting time. It is your responsibility to be at the starting line warmed up and ready to go on time. Don't blame the race organizers for the heavy traffic on the way to the race, the crowded parking lots, and the long lines at the toilets. Expect inconveniences.

• Try to do a little of every type of running in your warmup that you anticipate that you will do in the race, from start to finish — accelerating, pacing, sprinting.

• The warmup should last at least 15 minutes and should cover at least a mile.

If you time your warmup correctly — and of course the total time will depend upon your condition — you should complete the active phase 15 to 20 minutes before the start of the race. You should have ample time to towel off, change into dry racing clothes, perhaps change shoes, and have five minutes of complete rest (preferably lying down with your legs elevated). Then make a final visit to the bathroom and report to the start five minutes before the gun. Spend the last five minutes moving easily at a slow jog or a walk, and concentrating on the race.

I think that it is particularly important that you change into your racing uniform *after* your warmup, because this act will come to signify commitment, a sense that the "point of no return" has been reached, and thus help you prepare mentally for the race. Changing into racing flats has much the same effect. There is some argument, however, that you should warm up in racing flats to get used to their lighter weight before the competition starts. You might want to try both ways to see which helps your racing more.

PSYCHOLOGICAL ASPECTS

As your experience in competition grows, you will discover that the "spin-off" of the warmup into the psychological area becomes more and more pronounced. Your running buddies (and you too) will begin to display characteristic pre-race behavior.

During this phase many runners exhibit *competitive withdrawal obliv-ion*. In this state the runner *sees little* apart from the starting line of the race, *hears little* of anything that is said to him, and *remembers almost nothing* of the pre-race activities when questioned after the race. So don't be offended if a friend or acquaintance looks right through you while waiting for the race to start. Some become sporadic talkers, and are likely to make half a statement or half-answer a question before their conversation fades away. Because withdrawal oblivion seems to affect hearing, many who have the malady are thought ignorant, insensitive, or rude — sometimes all three.

Other runners are affected in the opposite manner, becoming ex-tremely gregarious. They crack jokes at the starting line and try to make lifelong friends of the runners they are lining up with.

Fortunately, most endurance runners fall between these extremes, and during their warmups are able to prepare for the physical and psychological demands of the race while still remaining in touch with their bodies and aware of their competitors.

Pacers and Racers

If you are intent upon running a specific time in your race, then there cannot be much strategy in your approach to racing. Simply stated, it doesn't matter what anyone else does — you're running against the clock, not against any other runners.

The way to finish in the time you've trained for is simple. On each schedule in Chapter 7 is the "mile split" for the time that that schedule prepared you for. For example, a 3:10 marathon has mile splits of 7:14: each mile of a three-hour ten-minute marathon will average seven minutes and fourteen seconds. The most efficient way to run any given time is to run "even splits" — run each mile at the same pace — and then sprint at the end of the race.

In certain circumstances it is also prudent to begin your race with a moderate sprint. For instance, if you're running on a course that starts on a wide street but narrows down to a jogging trail after a quarter of a mile, you need to get toward the front of the pack so that congestion won't interfere with your running even splits.

By and large, that's all the strategy a pacer needs. But what pacing lacks in strategy, it makes up for in effort, because the clock is the most implacable opponent you will ever face. "He who competes against time," wrote Samuel Johnson, "has an adversary who does not suffer casualty."

As your running continues to improve, there will be more and more times when you will want to be a "racer" rather than a "pacer." A racer is one who runs to beat another — to get an Olympic medal, to win an age-group award, or to get the last T-shirt of the 200 that are given out to race finishers.

The strategy involved in being a racer is infinitely more complex than simple pacing, and the rewards for learning the strategy proportionately greater. Time after time in the history of racing, runners with slower personal bests have beaten runners with faster PB's simply because they used superior race strategy. Look at Mary Decker's wins over the "faster" Soviet women in the 1983 World Championships, or Roger Bannister's victory over John Landy in the "Mile of the Century" at the 1954 Commonwealth Games.

Competitive Types: The "Front Runner" and the "Sitter"

The front runner is the extrovert of the track or road race. He expresses his emotions by competing with a high degree of visibility from the front of the pack. He is a person of action who enjoys the feeling of control he gets when forcing the pace from the front of the field, and he is happiest when relentlessly grinding an opponent or an entire field into submission.

Winning is important to the front runner, but he is sometimes more interested in the results of his *influence* during the race than in the eventual outcome. Thus front runners often become "rabbits," sought out by the super-elite to set a record-breaking pace, while the other runners "sit" and wait for the rabbit to drop out and the real racing to begin. But racers with the front-runner temperament sometimes cling to the notion that many a front runner has become a dominant force in endurance running — Paavo Nurmi, Emil Zatopek, Ron Clarke, Mary Decker, Craig Virgin — and hope to join that club.

The sitter usually has the temperament of the classic introvert, more interested in results rather than actions, and thus focuses on the win. Sitters are tenacious; they are the pit bulls of endurance running, and their strength lies in fastening on to a runner or a pack and defying anyone to dislodge them.

Sitters feel that they control the pace from the rear, that they are the shadow which drives the front runner to greater achievements. They are the race "employers" — the front runners are working for them, making their running task easier. They tend to train conscientiously, but are frequently secretive about their workouts. Many great runners have been sitters — Roger Bannister, Gordon Pirie, and Miruts Yifter.

A FRONT RUNNER VERSUS A SITTER

One of the classic confrontations between a front runner and a sitter took place in Melbourne, Australia, in the 10,000-meter final of the 1956 Olympics.

Gordon Pirie of Great Britain, tall, slim, and an experienced sitter, made no secret of his intention to destroy the competition in the last 200 meters. Vladimir Kuts's specialty was a series of gut-wrenching surges, which he would throw at his opponents from his favorite position in the front of the pack. The dour, heavily muscled Russian was sure that no man in the world could stay with him.

At the starting gun Kuts exploded into the lead, running his first lap on the soft and crumbling track in 62 seconds, daring the field to go with him. Pirie responded immediately, moving onto the Russian's shoulder, a position he would hold for lap after lap.

Approaching the 2-mile mark, Kuts swung wide and beckoned Pirie to come through to take the lead. The Englishman, adhering to his strategy, would have none of it. As if to punish him for failure to respond, Kuts burst forward with a hard sprint, Pirie following right behind. For the next two miles, Kuts surged hard every lap in an effort to demoralize his opponent. Still Pirie held his position on Kuts's shoulder.

Vladimir Kuts (center, in dark singlet), with Gordon Pirie following, about to lap former world-record holder Dave Stephens of Australia in the 1956 Olympic 10,000-meter final.

In the fifth mile, Kuts moved out three times and waved Pirie through. Every time the Englishman refused to be enticed.

In lap 21, with only one mile left in the race, Kuts again ran wide, then slowed so dramatically that Pirie was suddenly and apparently reluctantly forced to lead. Kuts dropped back to Pirie's shoulder, but several times in the next half-lap moved up even, as if trying to judge what Pirie had left in him.

Suddenly, Kuts burst past Pirie with the fastest and longest surge of the race. Although caught by surprise, Pirie responded immediately and managed to stay with Kuts for 200 meters. Then, exhausted, he lost ground — at first slowly, and then more quickly as he realized he had been broken. As the shadows lengthened across the Olympic stadium, Pirie was passed by several competitors — including me — and lost the Olympic medal he had been so confident of winning.

The year after the Melbourne Olympics I was often with Pirie on the European running circuit, and I asked him about his race against Kuts.

"It was torture, utter torture," Pirie said. "I didn't mind the defeat, in one way — it was just the way he did it. He simply murdered me! He must have been on drugs!"

It was still inconceivable to Gordon, like many sitters, that any human being could beat him from the front. For the rest of the tour whenever a journalist would ask him his world-record times at 3000 and 5000 meters, Pirie would always give the information — and add, "Without drugs!"

Competitive Types: The Tactician

If the front runner corresponds to the extrovert and the sitter to the introvert, the tactician is an ambivert, adapting his tactics to run from the front or the back, confusing his opponents with chameleonlike strategies.

When he goes to the front in an important race, it is not often to pick up the pace and grind his opponents into the ground, but to gain a tactical advantage by slowing *down* the pace subtly, while his opponents assume that by setting the pace he will wear himself out. The tactician always knows his maximum safe speed, and rarely burns himself out.

Frequently a tactician will choose a race which to him is unimportant and run it hard from the front all the way, just to keep his occasional "front-runner" posture believable. When asked about his race strategy, he will reply in typical front-runner clichés about "killing the kick of so-and-so" or "I needed free and unimpeded running."

Usually, however, a tactician is more at home running from the back of the lead pack, where he knows that his presence is disruptive. Not a true sitter, he will float up to the leader's shoulder, lurk around two or three places back, or throw in a few sharp bursts from the lead before falling back into the pack. The less experienced runners will conclude that he has been broken by the pace; the more experienced will suspect he's up to something, but no one knows his real strategy.

The tactician trades on his ability to orchestrate misjudgments and tactical errors on the part of his opponents. Although he frequently has extraordinary running ability, he would rather have his wins credited to his intelligence or to his smart racing tactics. Accordingly, his principal weakness is being outsmarted by another competitor who plays on the tactician's tendency to think that *he* is the only tactician in the race. While the tactician can accept defeat in competition, he can often find it hard to believe that the "biter" was bitten.

ELITE TACTICIANS

One of the greatest tactical performances in recent history came in the 5000- and 10,000-meter runs in the 1976 Montreal Olympics. Lasse Viren, another of the great runners that Finland seems to produce in disproportionate numbers, was forced into the tactician's role by a number of considerations. The first was that he had determined that he was going to run not only the 5000- and 10,000-meter runs, but the marathon as well. This meant that he needed to keep his energy expenditure as low as possible during the heats and finals he would run the first week so that he could tackle the grueling marathon on the last day of the Olympics. Second, it was likely that his competitors would use his 5000-meter heat and his 10,000-meter heat to assess his condition and tactics for the approaching finals. On the other hand, Viren was aided by the fact that, suffering from his usual post-Olympic slump, he had run very poorly since his two gold medals at Munich, so none of his competitors had had much recent experience racing against him.

Accordingly, in his heats Viren ran only fast enough to make sure he qualified: the top four in each heat advanced, and he was fourth each time. But in the finals of both races, he kept the other runners guessing, running far back in the pack, moving up, dropping back again, and taking the lead only once — when he could hold it to the end. Having made Olympic history with the first "double double" — both the 5000- and 10,000-meter gold medals in two consecutive Olympics — Viren ran the Olympic marathon as well. Here his tactic was obvious: stay with the leaders and hope that the heats and the finals hadn't taken too much out of his legs. Viren's eventual fourth place in the marathon capped a great performance.

The marathon offers even more opportunity than shorter races for the good tactician because there is not as much need to fear the "loss of contact" with the leaders. A strong runner who is sure of his pace can let the lead pack run away from him and destroy themselves — if the runner has made the right decision. If he's wrong, he's lost his chance of winning. Thus, because Ron Tabb had the reputation of going out too fast and burning out in his marathons, Bill Rodgers let him go at Boston in 1983. Rodgers later said that he thought, "He'll come back. He's just being an idiot." Tabb didn't come back that time, running 2:09:32 for second place.

The recent marathon career of Rob de Castella offers an interesting medley of marathon-winning tactics. In the 1981 Fukuoka Marathon, Rob stayed with the pack, which was towed by Garry Bjorklund at a sub-2:08 pace through 25 kilometers. There, incredibly, Bjorklund surged to a 70-yard lead. Gradually, over the next 5 kilometers, the pack ran Bjorklund down, and when they caught him, he crumbled. The fast pace took its toll among the pack too, and de Castella found himself being "sat on" by Takeshi Soh and Kunimitsu Itoh. By surging up a hill at 32 kilometers (about 20 miles) Rob dropped them both, and went on to win in 2:08:18 (five seconds behind Salazar's world-record time at New York, but the fastest ever on an out and back course and an impressive 1:18 faster than Derek Clayton's course record).

A similar situation at the Commonwealth Games in 1982 required a different solution. Early in the race the Tanzanians, Juma Ikangaa and Gidamis Shahanga, broke away from everyone, while de Castella remained with the second pack. By the half-marathon mark, Ikangaa had dropped his teammate, but showed no sign that the pace was wearing him out. Between 25 and 30 kilometers, de Castella decided that the pack was holding him back, and broke from it in pursuit of Ikangaa. At 30 kilometers, Ikangaa still had a 58-second lead over Rob, and many spectators doubted that de Castella could make up an entire minute in

10,000 meters to catch a runner like Ikangaa. He caught the Tanzanian at 39 kilometers, but Ikangaa did not crumble. The lead changed hands five times in the twenty-fifth mile, until de Castella's "speed through strength" training enabled him to take and hold the lead over the last mile to win by 12 seconds in 2:09:18. (Ikangaa ran 15:43 for the last 5000 meters; Rob 15:03.)

Obviously, de Castella had made exactly the right decision at exactly the right time. But knowing when to "jump" from the second pack and have a run at the leaders takes the finest judgment. You may go too early — Ron Clarke said after watching the 1982 Commonwealth Games Marathon, "When the Tanzanians broke away I'd have gone with them . . . and I would have died with them." Or you may go too late — most runners remember the Boston Marathon of 1978, when Jeff Wells surged hard for the last six miles of the race, only to come up nine seconds behind Bill Rodgers. Wells is probably one of the few marathon runners in history to wish that the distance were just a little greater, for he had mistimed his move by only a few seconds.

When the world's two fastest marathoners met in Rotterdam in 1983, everyone expected that Salazar and de Castella would go at it hammer and tongs for the entire 26 miles. In the actual event, however, Salazar left the pack when Rudolfo Gomez led for much of the race and pulled the pack through the five kilometers from 35 to 40K in 14:39. Gomez then couldn't handle the pace and dropped back. The pack had been cut to de Castella and Carlos Lopes of Portugal. The strategy for Lopes was obvious — a world-class 10,000-meter runner with a best 10K time of under 27:30, he clearly had more speed than Rob, whose best 10K was 28:12. Lopes sat. De Castella even eased the pace, but Lopes just slowed down and stayed on his shoulder. Rob, thus forced into the position of front runner, had to play the role for all it was worth: with 500 meters to go, he said, "I just put my head down and ran as fast as I could."

The last quarter of a mile was run in about 60 seconds, the last 5000 meters in 14:32, and de Castella won — this time as a front runner — by 2 seconds.

De Castella's races show his tactical sense — winning in Fukuoka by staying with the pack, leaving the pack to run down the leader in the Commonwealth Games, and winning the Rotterdam Marathon from the front. He would repeat the last tactic in Helsinki to win the 1983 World Championship.

You and the Competition

In longer races, you can frequently use the company of other runners to while away the time and make the miles pass easier. If the pace is slow enough to talk a little, as it can be occasionally in a marathon, and almost always is in ultra-marathons, some conversation can give the race the feeling of your regular long endurance run. Even when the pace is stiff enough so that no one feels like talking, the fact that you're in a pack makes it a lot easier to maintain the pace than it would be if you were alone.

Sooner or later, however, the pack is going to begin to break up, as the weaker runners fall off the pace. Here, in the closing stages of the race, when the legs are beginning to feel the pace and the breath is coming shorter, it is better *not* to listen to your body. Your body will be saying, "Quit." Your mind knows you just need to hang on a little bit longer. At this point, there are two ways to use the other runners to help you through.

If you're strong and moving well, concentrate on picking off the runners ahead of you as they tire. Sometimes you can do that even when you are as tired as they — this toughness is the hallmark that distinguishes the great athlete from the merely elite. But it is important to realize that mental toughness is not a factor of athletic ability; the middle-of-the-pack runner can be just as tough-minded as the super-elite. And while that toughness will not allow him to defeat the pack leaders, who surpass him in physical ability, it will make him the scourge of the many runners who can match his ability but lack his determination.

If, on the other hand, you're having one of those terrible races in which people are streaming past you in the last two miles, you can use the other runners to pull you in. Drop in behind someone who passes and run his pace as long as you can. When you have to let him go, drop your pace a little, count to twenty, and pick another runner to latch on to. In many ways the mental strength required to do this is greater than that needed to push the pace when you're running well — here you don't have the feeling of a good race to bolster you, and the periods of surging with the other runners always terminate in acute discomfort. When you get within 250 yards of the finish, start your sprint just as you normally would. Since it is anaerobic, your ability to sprint is not affected by the rest of your race. Because you are track-trained, you will probably find yourself catching some of those you had to let go a few minutes earlier.

There is one situation when it is *not* a good idea to latch onto another runner: when your pride is piqued by being passed by someone who "shouldn't" be ahead of you. Typically, the other runner is older or female; sometimes he just "runs funny." Whatever the reason, the runner who has been passed says, "I'm not going to let that @#%&* beat me in a race." He then speeds up, and runs ahead of the other until he grinds himself into the dust.

Even if you do manage to outrun the other, you have still abandoned your race pace and your carefully laid plans to defeat a runner who, if you're right, shouldn't be close to you anyway. At the worst of times, this macho mentality means that the top women runners have to weave their way through and around dying male runners who are damned if *they're* going to be beaten by a woman. Since elite women runners' performances consistently now come to within 15 percent of elite male performances, it is much smarter to run your own race and do your best. If someone shouldn't be ahead of you, he probably *won't* be at the end of the race — unless you kill yourself off. You might also remember that story of the 1956 Olympic 10,000 between Pirie and Kuts — a vivid example of what unplanned surges can do to race strategy.

You and Competitive Anxiety

One thing that can interfere with your ability to race — tactically or against the clock — is the anxiety which competition produces in runners. Even though you have mastered the elements of form and relaxed running techniques, and done all the training, if you allow anxiety to dominate your pre-race preparation and the race itself, you will fall short of your potential.

Such runners exist even at the national level. They are described by track commentators in various ways: "lots of talent, but no guts," they may say, or "lacks the killer instinct — looks great in training, but doesn't have it in competition."

While there do exist "competitive cripples" — runners with anxiety so great that they cannot compete — *most runners* with this problem have

Pat Clohessy winning the NCAA 3-mile in a record 13:47, June 1961.

simply never been taught how to handle competition anxiety. In fact, this anxiety can be turned to the runner's benefit, providing an energy source that, if controlled, can increase the ability to race.

I first became aware of the techniques for controlling competition anxiety while working with my fellow Australian Pat Clohessy. Both of us had come to the United States in 1958 to compete for the University of Houston. Pat's competitive performances during the first two years of his college career were competent but undistinguished. When, in my junior year, I ruptured my Achilles tendon and had to sit out a year of competition, Pat and I worked closely together to solve Pat's problem with anxiety.

To begin with, I had two misconceptions about competitive ability: that a runner either had it or he didn't, and that it could not be taught. I had forgotten, however, my own competitive anxiety during the first nine years that I ran. During that period when I worked with Pat, I realized that my own coach, Chicks Hensley, by using practical measures and psychological ploys, had taught me *how* to compete. Surprisingly, I had blocked out much of the agony of my first nine years of running with a big city club, and my "coming up" through the ranks.

Pat Clohessy had had a different background. He began running in his late teens without formal coaching, and he lived in isolated country towns far away from the big cities in Australia where track and field flourished. In spite of these drawbacks, however, he developed rather quickly, and he eventually joined my club, the Botany Harriers.

Although he showed obvious ability, his even more obvious nervousness before and after every race, fast or slow, usually resulted in his throwing up. His nickname among team members became "Super Spit" (Australian humor at that time was not noted for its subtlety).

Therefore, when I sat out the competition in 1961, both Pat and I knew what his problem was — excessive competition anxiety — and we worked together to figure out how to make him a more complete competitor.

We began by making a list of attributes that we felt were common to good competitors and, opposite them, a list of what we thought were deficiencies for runners in general, and Pat in particular. From this initial analysis, we began to synthesize the ideas we use today on how to compete effectively:

THE SEVEN RULES OF COMPETITIVE RUNNING

1. *Run even splits.* This immediately eliminates one practical reason for poor competitive performance, and allows the runner to concentrate on resolving the psychological aspects of his racing. (Pat had adopted the tactic of going out hard in every race so that he would be "competitive" with another Houston teammate and myself. Since the other teammate and I had a fierce rivalry in competition, we would frequently go out as hard as possible to burn each other out.) Once you are experienced enough to control race anxiety, you can begin to experiment with tactical racing.

2. *Realize that all runners suffer from race anxiety.* Once you understand that you're in the same boat with your competitors, you will see that the solution isn't to get rid of the anxiety (which is impossible) but to control it.

3. *Realize that concentrating on the positive can decrease the negative.* In Pat's case, we had him stop thinking about his own running problems and weaknesses, and concentrate instead on those of his opponents.

4. *Believe that consistent, commonsense training translates into successful racing.* If a runner does the preparation, he'll be physically ready to run the race — it's that simple.

5. *Never quit in a race* (unless, of course, you suffer injury). All runners have the desire, sometimes fleeting, sometimes constant, to drop out. Even champions have this feeling, but conquer it through fierce desire and resolute motivation.

6. *Accept that winning or losing does not make you a better or a worse person.* A bad race doesn't mean that you'll have to declare bankruptcy, lose your friends, never be invited to the White House, or be ridiculed.

7. *Even if you don't feel confident, fake it.* Time after time, I have seen a marginal runner act the role of confident competitor, and eventually become one.

Our rules changed Pat Clohessy into a competitor and an endurance runner of national caliber. In 1961, after a brilliant season of racing, he won the NCAA 3-mile championship, and successfully defended his title in 1962 to close out what had become an outstanding college career.

Pat Clohessy returned to Australia, where he competed on behalf of that nation in international competition. Currently he is the Australian national and Olympic distance coach. His top protégé is Rob de Castella, the 1983 world champion in the marathon.

SIX

Recovery

"HE HAS TO BE VERY CAREFUL not to overrace" — Rob de Castella on Alberto Salazar, April 1983.

How often have you heard that? Overracing is a problem and not just for the elite runner — in fact, the elite runner is more likely to know his own limitations (or at least have a coach who can keep him in line) than is the average self-coached athlete.

The amount of time you should leave between races varies according to the distance raced and your level of fitness, but one thing is true of most runners: if you ignore the necessary time your body needs to recover, then either injury or burnout will put you on the sidelines. The reluctance to take a day or two of light work, the hope instead that sustained hard training will give you an extra edge, can set you back weeks in your development program.

There is a general rule of coaching that a runner should allow time enough between similar-distance races to run regular workout mileage equal to the race distance times 10. Thus, after a marathon, the distance to run in your regular workouts would be $26.2 \times 10 = 262$ miles. On the other hand, a 10K runner would need only $6.2 \times 10 = 62$ miles of recovery before he could compete at that distance again.

This rule implies that an average runner who's doing about 70 miles a week could race a 10K two Saturdays in a row and suffer no ill effects. It is certainly true that well-trained college athletes regularly double at 5000 and 10,000 meters several weeks in succession during the track season.

However, the rule also implies that the same 70-mile-a-week runner could be ready to compete again in a marathon about a month after a hard marathon effort. This is almost certainly *not* true; even six weeks is too little time for most people, although there are still a lot of runners who think of a month and a half as a standard marathon recovery period. It is a sure road to burnout — unless you get injured first.

Most runners would probably see improvements in their times in the marathon if they ran *no more* than three a year — and even that is pushing it for many runners. If, year after year, your best marathon is the first one you run, and the next is slower, and the next one slower still, Mother Nature is talking to you. Listen; she gets angry when you don't.

If, on the other hand, your best marathon time comes in the second or third effort of the year, experiment with skipping the first one or "running through it" easily as a training run. To keep your mind in shape for racing, compete occasionally at shorter distances, remembering that any competitive effort over 30K will make a bigger withdrawal from your "running account" than you can replace in a few weeks or a month.

The following section deals primarily with *marathon* recovery, because nothing places the tremendous stresses on the mind and body that marathon racing does. The principles of recovery are the same for shorter races, and the recovery techniques are equally effective for them. Because of the shorter duration of stress in the shorter races, recovery will be relatively quicker — except perhaps late in the season, when week after week of hard racing can wear you down almost to the post-marathon level.

The Battered-Mind Syndrome

Most endurance runners understand that the marathon extracts an immediate physical and psychological price from each competitor, but, as a self-coached runner, you should understand as well that the trauma of marathon running extends far beyond the normal limits of competition.

The physical toll is far easier to assess. Nearly every marathon runner has a favorite story about heat problems in Phoenix, a stress fracture in

New York, a hamstring pull on Heartbreak Hill in Boston, and so on. Physical ailments have a way of commanding the endurance runner's attention, especially after the adrenaline of the racing effort has worn off.

But the mental strain of running a competitive marathon is no more the exclusive worry of the elite runners in the front pack than is the danger of physical injury. In fact, because of the "tactical" nature of many important races, the leaders are frequently running at a smaller percentage of their capabilities than are the mid-pack runners who — running against the clock in pursuit of a personal record — must push themselves from the gun. Perhaps for the reasons mentioned in Chapter 2, the marathon itself evokes greater emotional feelings from its participants than any other event in track and field. It is not unusual to see runners emerge from the marathon either on a mental "high" or extremely depressed.

Most of the tears and accompanying depression result from disappointment in race performance, combined with the stress of intense concentration for three, four, or five hours, which in turn is the culmination of weeks and months of intense mental and physical preparation. I call this post-marathon depression the "Battered-Mind Syndrome."

While it is impossible to avoid the mental stresses attendant upon running a marathon, there are a number of commonsense rules you can follow to avoid the battered-mind syndrome:

- Set realistic goals. Don't just pick a time you *hope* you can run.
- Modify your race expectations to fit the particular conditions on race day — the human body slows down in heat, cold, humidity, and wind, but the stopwatch does not.
- Do not allow overt or implied pressure from your friends, running buddies, or competitors to alter *your* race plans.
- If you are running your first marathon, OR you are relatively inexperienced, OR you are short on conditioning, *be content to finish the distance*.

Attention to these aspects of marathon racing — and the standards in the schedules — will enable you to make your marathons rewarding and satisfying experiences, from which your "battered mind" will soon recover.

Physical Recovery

The first step to physical recovery from a marathon is to accept that your body has been punished by an endurance effort of this length. Pay no attention to the stories you may hear from your running buddies about somebody who played two hours of touch football the morning after a marathon; you're probably not going to feel like it. Even if you DO feel like it, DON'T do it.

Your recovery from the marathon begins the moment you step across the finish line. Resist the temptation to lie down; you need to keep moving to pump the products of fatigue out of your muscles. If they remain there, not only will you be sore the next two or three days, but you may increase your chance of injury during the following week.

Begin immediately to drink — ideally something cold with caffeine, like a cola, in hot weather; coffee or tea in cold weather. This is also a good time to take two aspirin tablets, if your stomach can handle it. Aspirin not only helps relieve the immediate discomfort of your effort but also helps reduce the inflammation in your muscles and tendons that can lead to further discomfort and a slower recovery. A lot of runners, awed by the marathon experience and elated by their success, head immediately for the free beer often provided by the race organizers. A beer may be a nice social conclusion to balance the essential loneliness of the long-distance run, but a lot of beer on an empty stomach can combine with the body's physical aches and pains to produce a hangover more memorable than the race itself.

As soon as it is practical, take a warm to moderately hot bath, soaking the legs thoroughly. While soaking, gently massage the entire length of the leg with emphasis on the calves, the quadriceps, and any other muscle groups that feel fatigued. Use a firm stroking and kneading action, always working toward the heart. After bathing, dress warmly, and when you feel that you have gained a measure of strength back, go for a walk. That evening, repeat the bath and the short walk, and add light stretching.

The day following the marathon should include warm baths, gentle stretching, and thirty minutes of easy jogging. The jogging will stimulate circulation in your punished muscles and thus help remove residual fatigue products. The rehabilitation of stiff and sore hyperfatigued muscles has now begun in earnest.

The second day after the marathon, repeat the regimen above.

Post-marathon days three, four, and five should not include jogging — only walking and stretching. On these days, concentrate on getting enough sleep and on replacing minerals and trace elements you have almost certainly lost during the race.

Remember that for a full week after your marathon, the emphasis is on recovering, not training. Training should not resume at even a modest level until the second week — always assuming that you have not sustained an injury either in the marathon or in the post-marathon week. (It is possible to get injured even when you're jogging during the week after.)

Be aware that the mind usually recovers more quickly after a marathon than does the body, even when you experience the battered-mind syndrome. Consequently, it is very easy to resume your normal training faster than advisable, and this accounts in large part for the high numbers of injuries and illnesses reported by runners after marathons.

Do not resume normal training levels until the third week after a marathon. Even then you will occasionally notice "dead legs," flatness, and tiredness in your workouts. Be alert for these signs and don't attempt to push through them. Modify your training instead, and *never,* NEVER use other marathoners as a gauge of how you should feel.

Elite runners can sometimes get away with superb marathons only weeks apart, but even among the elite, this is an exception, not the general rule. Most very good runners can get "up" for only three marathons a year. The average aspiring runner usually finds two well-spaced marathons per year enough to handle successfully.

Recovery from Shorter Races

Obviously, there is usually less physical trauma during and after 10K and 10-mile races than after a marathon. On the other hand, a race at these shorter distances can be physically stressful, and this stress is compounded if the shorter race is *the* race for which you've trained for months, by a mental letdown much like the battered-mind syndrome.

It is therefore advisable to treat recovery from a very hard 10K or 10-mile race cautiously, even though you will not need the full period of post-marathon recovery. After a hard shorter race, it is a good idea to jog easily for the following two days, and then to take the third post-race day off entirely. Use this day to evaluate how you feel. If you still feel tired, burned out, or simply not very motivated, jog easily for the rest of the week. If, on the other hand, you feel eager to return to training, do so on the fourth post-race day.

"Training Through" a Race

Occasionally in the training schedules you will see that a runner has run a race in the middle of a schedule without taking any time for post-race recovery. In a few cases, these "trained-through" races are full-length marathons.

If you would like to "train through" a race in your own schedule, remember that such a race can be run hard, but should not be raced "all-out." Try to keep your effort about the same as it would be for a strength run.

If the race you would like to train through is a marathon, you need to be especially cautious. Even an easy pace can become very hard to hold by 20 miles, and you don't want to harm your chances of being ready when the race you're training toward comes around. It's usually wise to set a maximum speed that you will not exceed during the marathon. Best-marathon pace plus 30 seconds a mile seems to be safe for most people. By observing these guidelines, you can use a race as a long strength run and also get some extra experience in competition to help prepare you for the big day.

SEVEN

The Schedules

THE SCHEDULES IN THIS CHAPTER are divided into three distinct groups, corresponding to the most popular distances raced in this country. First are the schedules for 10K road races and 10,000-meter track races. The schedules provide workouts for athletes training to run 10K races of 30, 32, 34, 36, 38, 40, 42:30, 45, 47:30, 50, 52:30, and 55 minutes. The second group prepares the runner for races in the range of ten miles — 15K (9.3 miles), 10 miles, 20K (12.4 miles), and the half-marathon (13.1 miles). For the sake of simplicity and ease of use, the schedules are grouped according to times attainable in 10-mile races: 50, 55, 60, 65, 70, 75, 80, 85, and 90 minutes (the pace ranges from 5 minutes per mile to 9 minutes per mile). The last group of schedules is devoted to training the prospective marathon runner. He or she can prepare for marathons of 2:20, 2:30, 2:40, 2:50, 3:00, 3:10, 3:20, 3:30, 3:45, and 4:00. A final schedule is provided for the person who wishes to run a "survival" marathon, with no time goal.

Using the Schedules

If you are working with a structured schedule for the first time, you will experience a certain amount of variation in your capabilities from day to day.

• There will be days when you breeze through a workout; it feels like "child's play." Good. That means you are getting stronger, and it may also mean that that particular workout is very well suited to your running abilities at that moment. *Do not* assume that this workout means that you can jump to a more difficult schedule: it always takes more than one good workout (and often takes more than one good race) to justify a big move.

• There will be days when you say, "This workout on the schedule is so easy that there's no point in doing it." If you give in to that impulse, you will find yourself a little short on race day. Also, *do not* try to "improve" the workout by cutting 10 seconds a lap off it — you may be able to complete it, but it may leave you flat for an important workout coming up.

• There will also be days when you try to do the workout and it is simply beyond your capabilities on that day. Try to run it within the time limitations set out in the section below. If you cannot do so, go on to the section, "Saving a Workout."

Schedule Paces and Times

If you are not accustomed to running paced track work, you will probably have some problems with pace judgment. As you gain experience, your pace judgment will improve quickly, but it will take many laps around the track, and several years of running, before you can hit your intervals to the second, time after time, as the more experienced elite runners can.

Fortunately, such precision is not necessary. On the other hand, if we accept the fact that you're not going to be exactly on pace every lap, the question becomes, "How close is close enough? If I'm supposed to run a 6:00 mile and I run a 6:12, is that okay, or should I do it over?"

The following guidelines provide some help in relating the times you are *supposed* to run to the times that you *actually* run:

For distances UP TO AND INCLUDING 1 MILE, you may exceed or fall short of the scheduled times up to *4 seconds per quarter.** Thus each workout on the schedule falls into a range of acceptable times:

> 3 × 1 mile in 6:00** = 3 × 1 mile in 5:44 to 6:16 (4 seconds × 4 quarters in 1 mile = a 16-second range)
> 5 × 880 in 2:50 = 5 × 880 in 2:42 to 2:58 (4 seconds × 2 quarters in a half-mile = an 8-second range)

*If you are unused to track work and are uncertain about the meanings of terms like "quarter," "220," and so on, see page 205.

**One mile completed in 6 minutes, run 3 times.

12 × 220 in 39 seconds = 12 × 220 in 37 to 41 seconds (4 seconds × .5 quarter = a 2-second range)

For distances OVER ONE MILE, you may exceed or fall short of the
scheduled times by 2 *seconds per quarter*:

2 × 3 miles in 18:00 = 2 × 3 miles in 17:36 to 18:24 (12 quarters ×
2 seconds = a 24-second range)
3 × 1.5 miles in 8:30 = 3 × 1.5 miles in 8:18 to 8:42 (6 quarters ×
2 seconds = a 12-second range)

EXCEEDING OR FALLING SHORT OF SCHEDULE PACES AND TIMES

The guidelines above provide a substantial amount of "cushion" in adapting the times written on the schedules to the times you run on the track.
If you still consistently run faster or slower than the scheduled interval
times, including the built-in cushion, there are other factors that you
need to think about.

If, for several workouts in a row, you are *faster* than the schedule calls
for:

• Consider the possibility that you have underestimated your ability —
but do not jump immediately to a more advanced schedule.

• Consider that you might be making a very common mistake of inexperienced runners, killing yourself on the track. Intense effort in
workouts, day after day, will not make you faster; it will only slow your
races.

• If you are *sure* that you are not pushing too hard in workouts — if,
for instance, your heart rate stays around 170 even when you run your
intervals much too fast — move cautiously on to the next most advanced
schedule. Be alert for any sign of overtraining in the following weeks.

If, on the other hand, you are *slower* than the schedules call for,
consistently falling out of the allowable range of times, even though
you're running hard:

• Consider the possibility that you have overestimated your ability —
but do not immediately jump to an easier schedule.

• Consider all the possible reasons that you can't run your workout
times:

Are you coming back after time off, illness, injury?

Are you encountering a period of abnormal weather (heat wave,
extreme cold, continuous rain, strong winds)?

Are you overraced?

Are you overtrained?

Are you experiencing emotional stress at home?

Are you experiencing heavy job or academic pressure?

If the answer to any of these questions is "Yes," and you feel that conditions will remain that way for some time, you might want to move to an easier schedule. If you feel that conditions are temporary, refer to the next section.

Saving a Workout

The workouts that seem to need to be salvaged most often are those which involve continued stress for longer than ten minutes or so. Three times a mile with an 880 recovery, for example, is one that defeats a lot of runners, while repeat 440's or 220's never seem to be much of a problem, barring injury. Typically, on a day when you're going to have trouble, you'll begin to struggle early, having to work hard to get the first mile in the required time, and then, after the recovery, you'll have trouble running the correct pace even for the first lap of the next mile. You may swear and step off the track at this point, convinced that you're not a runner.

This is the time to save the workout. Immediately begin to jog a recovery half-mile, planning to complete the day with 2 × 440 with a quarter-mile recovery jog, and then 2 × 220 with a 220 jog. The times to shoot for in your quarters should be about 5 to 7 seconds per lap faster than your mile pace was, and your 220's should be about 2 to 3 seconds faster than your 440 pace. For example, if you blew up doing repeat 6:00 miles (a pace of 90 seconds per 440), the conclusion to "save" the workout would be 2 × 440 in 83–85 seconds, followed by 2 × 220 in 38–40 seconds.

Concluding the workout this way has several advantages: first, you get some real work to put on your training calendar instead of writing "dropped out." Second, the faster pace, instead of being more tiring, will usually "wake you up" a little — you're likely to feel better after the 220's than you did before the workout began. Third, you have learned something you can use in a race: when you felt you couldn't run another lap at 90 seconds, you were actually capable of running nearly another mile at a significantly faster pace. When Keats wrote about how "the dull brain perplexes and retards," he was talking about more than the operation of the poetic fancy: a runner's mental limits are usually reached before his physical limits.

"Optimum" versus "Modified" Schedules

Occasionally in the training schedules you will find two schedules side by side, one called "optimum" and one called "modified." The "optimum" schedule is the one you should try to follow, since it gives you the better training. Occasionally the runners doing the training were forced to modify their workouts because of work, injury, weather, other racing commitments, or other factors. Their modifications are shown where they occurred, and illustrate that even drastic changes in a few days' (or even a week's) training will *not* destroy your chances of achieving your goals. (When only one schedule appears, it is the "optimum" schedule.)

Schedule Terminology

In most places the exact pace of a given workout has been spelled out. If you are new to track training, though, you might benefit from definitions of a few terms:

STRIDES are short intervals in which you run fast but with control — not an all-out sprint that leaves you breathless. Concentrate here on good form and quick rhythm (sometimes called "turnover") rather than on working hard.

STRENGTH RUNS are faster-paced runs of several miles in the middle of longer, slower runs. Thus you may see on the schedule a notation, "15 miles incorporating 6 miles in 36:00." This means that at some point in your 15-mile run for that day you will pick up the pace to 6 minutes per mile and run 6 miles at that pace without stopping. The remainder of your run will consist of "easy running."

EASY RUNNING varies according to the runner's ability, and so the range of acceptable times for this type of running is always given at the beginning of each schedule.

RECOVERY is the amount of distance you may jog between fast intervals. It should be a comfortable, slow pace; it can be almost as slow as walking, but you should maintain at least jogging form — i.e., don't walk; jog.

A TIME TRIAL is a workout in which you run a given distance as fast as you can.

If you are unused to track terminology, such as "220's," "quarters," and so on, see page 205.

The Warmup

Every track workout should be preceded by a warmup, which prepares the body for the stresses of the faster running and helps prevent injury. As mentioned in Chapter 5, regular use of a pre-workout warmup can also be useful in developing a psychological race-readiness.

While you will develop the right warmup for yourself by trial and error as you gain experience, here is a basic warmup for the self-coached runner who has not given much previous thought to this aspect of the sport:

1. Walk for 5 minutes or 440 yards.
2. Run for one mile in progressively faster 440-yard segments. For example, jog the first 440 in 3 minutes, the second in 2:30, the third in 2 minutes, and in the fourth quarter add 4 × 55-yard strides, with a 55-yard recovery jog between strides.
3. Do 5 to 10 minutes of easy stretching (stretch slowly; don't bounce):
   · Lower-leg stretches. Standing a few feet away from a firm, stable object (a tree, a wall, or a telephone pole is traditional), lean slightly forward and brace both arms against the object. Then move one foot a few feet behind the other, put the ball of that foot on the ground, and slowly push your heel down until it touches the ground. You should feel stretching along the back of the lower leg and in the Achilles tendon. Repeat with other leg.

- Heel raises. While standing on both feet, raise heels, then lower. Repeat 12 to 20 times.
- Posterior thigh (hamstring) stretches. While standing, touch your left foot with your right hand, moving slowly, keeping your left knee straight and moving your left arm up and back. Return to upright position, and reverse motion, moving your left hand to your right foot. Repeat 12 to 20 times on each side.
- Anterior thigh (quadriceps) stretches. Grasp your right leg with your left hand and pull your foot up to your buttocks; hold for 5 seconds and release. Repeat with left leg. Repeat 8 times for each leg.

  More easy stretching of your preference may follow.

4. Jog another 440, and then begin another short routine of non-explosive, modified sprint starts: leaning well forward, walk 3 or 4 steps, and then begin to run, increasing the pace every 5 steps until you reach a fast, controlled sprint. Repeat 3 times.
5. Jog another 440 yards, and then run 220 yards at anticipated race pace.
6. Jog or walk a final 440 yards.

The Warmdown

All track workouts should conclude with a warmdown, which prevents soreness by allowing the blood to remove by-products of hard exercise from the stressed muscles. Slow jogging for at least a mile is a good warmdown. If your workout was run in spikes, you should change into training flats and consciously press your heels onto the track to stretch out your Achilles tendons.

Conversion Factors

The following information will enable you to train for a race other than 10K, 10 miles, or marathon by modifying an existing schedule. You should have little or no trouble making the transition to other distances, but remember: listen to your body and use common sense (as you should do with any schedule).

- To train for a *5K race,* modify your 10K schedule as follows:
  1. Decrease your paced runs ("strength runs") to ⅔ distance, and increase pace 10–12 seconds per mile.
  2. Run your track work 2–3 seconds per 440 faster, and decrease the number of repetitions to ⅔ or ¾ of those called for on the 10K schedule.
- To train for a race at *15 miles, 25K, or 30K,* follow your marathon schedule, but plan on racing 10–15 seconds per mile faster.
- To train for ultra-marathon runs of *50K and 50 miles,* use the marathon schedule, and:
  1. For 50K, increase stamina runs to 24 miles.
  2. For 50 miles, add two 30-mile stamina runs eight and five weeks before your race, and one 35-miler three weeks before.

And finally, before beginning any of these training schedules, be sure to have a full examination by your physician.

Note: in all the schedules, "Day 1" is assumed to be a Sunday.

SCHEDULES FOR

Ten Kilometers

"'Odd's pittikins! Can it be six mile yet?"
—CYMBELINE

The 30-Minute 10K

You are ready to train for a 30-minute 10K if you can run:

220 yards in 28 seconds
440 yards in 59 seconds
1 mile in 4 minutes 14 seconds

To run 10K in 30 minutes you need to average 4:51 per mile.

An eight-week base of 70 to 90 miles weekly should be undertaken before the runner begins the eight-week schedule leading to the 30–minute 10K goal. A typical week should consist of:

- one long stamina run of 13 to 16 miles at 6:30 to 7:15 per mile
- two endurance workouts on the track (interval 440's, 880's, or single miles, all slightly faster than anticipated race pace)
- one medium-distance run (8 to 12 miles) with 6 to 10 strides of 60 to 130 yards, run at a fast and controlled pace
- three days of medium-distance (8 to 12 miles) maintenance runs at 6:30 to 7:15 per mile.

A 30-minute 10K belongs to the elite group of distance runners, and only a small percentage of athletes achieve this mark in their careers. Runners who belong in this category are highly motivated and disciplined and have the physiological and competitive ability to complement those qualities. This level of ability is just below the level of international competition, and once a runner reaches it he (at this point in athletic history, the 30-minute 10K is the sole dominion of males) usually makes the commitment that his sport will come first in his life until his ambitions are fulfilled — or he realizes that he is not going to be one of the very few on top of the mountain.

Our subject is Randy, a twenty-two-year-old runner, who graduated from college in the spring of 1983. After a brief rest from running, he began a summer buildup of 70 to 90 miles a week, much of it at a 6-minute pace. The rest of his training followed the standards set above. We pick up his final eight weeks of training before his attempt to run 30 minutes.

"Easy running" in this schedule is 6:30 to 7:15 per mile.

1st Week
Day

1 A.M. 4 miles easy running incorporating 6 × 120 (fast and controlled)
  P.M. 12 × 220 in 32 — 440 R*
2 A.M. 4 miles easy running incorporating 6 × 100 (fast and controlled)
  P.M. 10 miles easy running
3 A.M. 4 miles easy running incorporating 8 × 75 (fast and controlled)
  P.M. 12 × 440 in 80 — 110 R
4 A.M. 4 miles easy running incorporating 6 × 120 (fast and controlled)
  P.M. 12 miles easy running
5 A.M. 4 miles easy running incorporating 10 × 60 (fast and controlled)
  P.M. 6 miles easy running
6 6 miles easy running
7 13 miles easy running

2nd Week
Day

1 15 miles easy running
2 A.M. 5 miles easy running incorporating 6 × 130 (fast and controlled)
  P.M. 4 × 1 mile in 5:00 — 660 R
3 A.M. 3 miles easy running incorporating 4 × 120 (fast and controlled)
  P.M. 6 miles easy running
4 A.M. 4 miles easy running incorporating 8 × 85 (fast and controlled)
  P.M. 10 × 440 in 75 — 440 R
5 A.M. 4 miles easy running incorporating 3 × 150 (fast and controlled)
  P.M. 5 miles easy running
6 8 miles easy running
7 12 miles easy running incorporating 3 miles in 15:00

3rd Week
Day

1 A.M. 4 miles easy running incorporating 5 × 130 (fast and controlled)
  P.M. 6 × 880 in 2:30 — 440 R
2 A.M. 4 miles easy running incorporating 8 × 60 (fast and controlled)
  P.M. 9 miles easy running
3 A.M. 4 miles easy running incorporating 5 × 130 (fast and controlled)
  P.M. 6 miles easy running
4 A.M. 3 miles easy running incorporating 6 × 110 (fast and controlled)
  P.M. 6 × 330 in 50 — 110 R
5 10 miles easy running
6 6 miles easy running
7 15 miles easy running

4th Week
Day

1 12 miles easy running incorporating 2 × 3 miles in 16:00
2 A.M. 4 miles easy running incorporating 6 × 120 (fast and controlled)
  P.M. 12 × 220 in 33 — 220 R
3 A.M. 3 miles easy running incorporating 3 × 150 (fast and controlled)
  P.M. 10 miles easy running
4 A.M. 4 miles easy running incorporating 4 × 130 (fast and controlled)
  P.M. 8 × 880 in 2:25 — 220 R
5 A.M. 4 miles easy running incorporating 6 × 60 (fast and controlled)
  P.M. 6 miles easy running
6 6 miles easy running
7 15 miles easy running incorporating 10 miles in 59:00

*Run 200 yards in 32 seconds, 12 times, with a 440-yard recovery in between.

5th Week
Day

1   12 miles easy running incorporating 6 miles in 33:00
2   A.M. 4 miles easy running incorporating 4 × 120 (fast and controlled)
    P.M. 9 miles easy running
3   A.M. 4 miles easy running incorporating 8 × 50 (fast and controlled)
    P.M. 6 miles easy running
4   A.M. 3 miles easy running incorporating 5 × 100 (fast and controlled)
    P.M. 4 × 220 in 32 — 220 R; jog 660; 4 × 440 in 64 — 220 R; jog 660; 4 × 220 in 32 — 220 R
5   A.M. 3 miles easy running incorporating 2 × 150 (fast and controlled)
    P.M. 9 miles easy running
6   5 miles easy running
7   10K race in 30:14

6th Week

Day

1   10 miles easy running
2   A.M. 4 miles easy running incorporating 6 × 120 (fast and controlled)
    P.M. 16 × 110 in 15 — 330 R
3   6 miles easy running
4   A.M. 4 miles easy running incorporating 5 × 80 (fast and controlled)
    P.M. 20 × 440 in 74 — 220 R
5   A.M. 4 miles easy running incorporating 6 × 60 (fast and controlled)
    P.M. 6 miles easy running
6   Rest day
7   18 miles in 1:48:00

7th Week
Day

1   A.M. 4 miles easy running

incorporating 4 × 80 (fast and controlled)
    P.M. 9 miles easy running
2   12 miles easy running
3   A.M. 4 miles easy running incorporating 8 × 60 (fast and controlled)
    P.M. 4 × 330 in 46 — 110 R; jog 880; 4 × 330 in 46 — 110 R; jog 880; 4 × 330 in 46 — 110 R
4   A.M. 4 miles easy running incorporating 4 × 120 (fast and controlled)
    P.M. 4 × 660 in 1:34 — 660 R
5   A.M. 3 miles easy running incorporating 2 × 150 (fast and controlled)
    P.M. 5 miles easy running
6   5 miles easy running
7   8K race in 23:11

8th Week

Day

1   15 miles easy running
2   A.M. 4 miles easy running incorporating 3 × 130 (fast and controlled)
    P.M. 12 × 110 in 16 — 330 R
3   A.M. 4 miles easy running incorporating 6 × 60 (fast and controlled)
    P.M. 9 miles easy running incorporating 2 miles in 10:30
4   A.M. 4 miles easy running incorporating 3 × 80 (fast and controlled)
    P.M. 4 × 1 mile in 4:50 — 440 R
5   A.M. 4 miles easy running incorporating 6 × 110 (fast and controlled)
    P.M. 4 miles easy running
6   6 miles easy running
7   Rest day

9th Week

Day

1   Pro-Comfort 10K race in 29:14

The 32-Minute 10K

You are ready to train for a 32-minute 10K if you can run:

220 yards in 29 seconds
440 yards in 62 seconds
1 mile in 4 minutes 30 seconds

To run 10K in 32 minutes you need to average 5:08 per mile.

A 32-minute 10K requires a dedicated and consistent approach to training by a hard-working, talented runner. An eight-week base of 60 to 80 miles a week is necessary before beginning the final pre-race eight-week countdown leading to the 32-minute 10K. A typical training week during the "base" period should consist of:

- one long stamina run of 12 to 15 miles at 6:45 to 7:30 per mile
- two medium-distance runs of 7 to 10 miles with 4 to 8 strides of 60 to 130 yards, run at a fast and controlled pace
- one endurance workout on the track (interval 220's, 440's, 880's, or single miles, all slightly faster than anticipated race pace)
- three days of medium-distance (7 to 10 miles) maintenance runs at 6:45 to 7:30 per mile.

After this foundation has been established, you are ready for the final eight weeks of specialized training. During this particular eight-week period we will follow the training of Terry, a twenty-five-year-old salesman. Terry had attended a major university on a track scholarship and had run the steeplechase. He had been inactive for several years after graduation, but had resumed moderate training several months before his eight-week foundation phase.

"Easy running" in this schedule is 7:00 to 8:00 per mile.

1st Week

Day

1 15 miles easy running
2 2 × 2 miles in 10:45 — 1–mile R*
3 10 miles easy running incorporating 6 × 130 (fast and controlled)
4 6 × 880 in 2:30 — 440 R

5 10 miles easy running incorporating 6 × 130 (fast and controlled)
6 10 miles easy running
7 10 miles easy running incorporating 6 miles in 34:00

2nd Week
Day

1 18 miles easy running
2 6 × 440 in 65 — 660 R
3 8 miles easy running
   incorporating 6 × 130 (fast and
   controlled)
4 3 × 1 mile in 5:10 — 440 R
5 16 × 440 in 80 — 220 R
6 10 miles easy running
   incorporating 6 × 130 (fast and
   controlled)
7 10 miles easy running
   incorporating 6 miles in 34:00

3rd Week
Day

1 15 miles easy running
2 10 miles easy running
   incorporating 6 × 130 (fast and
   controlled)
3 20 × 440 in 80 — 220 R
4 10 miles easy running
   incorporating 6 × 130 (fast and
   controlled)
5 10 miles easy running
6 2 sets of 4 × 330 in 45 — 110
   between repetitions and 880
   between sets
7 10 miles easy running

4th Week
Day

1 18 miles easy running
2 440 in 70, 880 in 2:30, ¾ mile in
   3:55, 1 mile in 5:15 — all 440 R;
   jog 880; 1 mile in 5:00; ¾ mile in
   3:40, 880 in 2:20, 440 in 65 — all
   440 R
3 10 miles easy running
   incorporating 4 × 130 (fast and
   controlled)
4 12 × 220 in 32 — 220 R
5 10 miles easy running
6 6 miles easy running
7 Competition: 5K to 15K (Terry
   competed in a 5K race: 15:28)

5th Week
Day

1 15 miles easy running
2 12 × 440 in 75 — 220 R
3 4 × 1 mile in 5:20 — 660 R
4 10 miles easy running
   incorporating 5 × 130 (fast and
   controlled)
5 8 miles easy running
6 10 miles easy running
   incorporating 6 × 130 (fast and
   controlled)
7 8 × 880 in 2:30 — 220 R

6th Week
Day

1 18 miles easy running
2 16 × 220 in 32 — 220 R
3 10 miles easy running
4 2 × 2 miles in 10:30 — 880 R
5 10 miles easy running
   incorporating 6 × 130 (fast and
   controlled)
6 4 miles easy running
7 Competition: 5K to 15K (Terry
   competed in a 5K race: 15:05)

7th Week
Day

1 15 miles easy running
2 16 × 110 in 15 — 330 R
3 2 × 1.5 miles in 7:20 — 880 R
4 10 miles easy running
   incorporating 6 × 130 (fast and
   controlled)
5 Rest day
6 6 miles easy running
7 12 miles easy running
   incorporating 6 × 130 (fast and
   controlled)

8th Week
Day

1   15 miles easy running
2   16 × 440 in 80 — 110 R
3   2 × 2 miles in 11:00 — 660 R
4   6 miles easy running
    incorporating 4 × 130 (fast and
    controlled)
5   Rest day
6   3 miles easy running
7   Bayou City 10K: 31 minutes 35
    seconds

The 34-Minute 10K

For comparative purposes we are utilizing three training schedules for the 34-minute 10K examples. The "Optimum" schedule illustrates the ideal situation that we trust most runners find themselves in when they begin a specific training program for a specific event.

Ideally, the runner who is attempting the 34-minute 10K will have eight weeks of preliminary conditioning covering 50 to 70 miles weekly. This preliminary training should include the following components each week:

- one long stamina run of 12 to 15 miles at 7:30 to 8:00 per mile
- one endurance workout on the track (interval 440's, 880's, or single miles, all slightly faster than anticipated race pace)
- one medium-distance run (5 to 9 miles) with 4 to 8 medium strides of 60 to 130 yards, run at a fast and controlled pace
- four days medium-distance (5 to 9 miles) maintenance runs at 7:30 to 8:00 per mile.

Two case histories are also included to illustrate some puzzling phenomena that can occur in endurance training and racing. Runner A and Runner B are both attempting to run a sub–34:00 10K. Both are trained by the same coach; however, they differ in the foundation — or preliminary conditioning — phase of their preparation and in the final eight-week period of training and racing.

Runner A is coming off a base of marathon preparation and has just raced a marathon at the start of his 10K training. Runner B has spent the last two months on the track, preparing to run the National Master's Championships at 800 meters and 1500 meters. A lower back injury has caused a change in his plans, and he is now preparing for the 10K although he has averaged only 30 miles a week for the past eight weeks.

Runner A has run several sub–34:00 10K's, but the most recent was two years before this attempt. Runner B has a personal best of 34:15, run three years earlier. Both runners have met the criteria necessary to run 34:00.

"Easy running" in all examples below is 7:30 to 8:30 per mile.

Optimum Schedule	Runner A	Runner B

Optimum Schedule

1st Week

Day
1. 15 miles easy running
2. 2 × 2 miles in 11:00 — 1-mile R**
3. 10 miles easy running
4. 6 × 880 in 2:40 — 440 R
5. 10 miles easy running with 6 × 130 (fast and controlled)
6. 10 miles easy running
7. 10 miles incorporating 6 miles in 35:00

2nd Week

Day
1. 15 miles easy running
2. 6 × 440 in 68 — 660 R
3. 6 miles easy running
4. 3 × 1 mile in 5:20 — 660 R
5. Rest day
6. 16 × 440 in 82 — 220 R
7. 10 miles incorporating 6 miles in 35:00

*In post-marathon recovery phase (see recovery section in Chapter 6).
**Run 2 miles in 11 minutes, 2 times, with a 1-mile recovery in between.

Runner A

*1st Week**

Day
1. Houston Marathon: 2:39:59
2. 3 miles easy jog
3. 3 miles easy jog
4. Rest day
5. Rest day
6. Rest day
7. 6 miles easy jog

*2nd Week**

Day
1. 10 miles easy running
2. 10 × 220 in 40 — 440 R
3. 6 miles easy running
4. 4 × 440 in 75 — 440 R
5. Rest day
6. 6 miles with 6 × 65 (fast and controlled)
7. 10 miles easy running

Runner B

1st Week

Day
1. Rest day
2. 8 × 440 in 81 — 110 R
3. 8 miles easy running
4. 660 in 1:35, 330 in 41, 220 in 27 — all 660 R
5. 9 miles incorporating 6 miles in 39:00
6. Rest day
7. Rest day

2nd Week

Day
1. 6 miles in 42:00
2. 3 × 550 in 1:26, 440 in 68 — all 440 R
3. 9 miles easy running
4. 2 × 2 miles in 12:45 — 440 R
5. 6 miles with 4 × 120 (fast and controlled)
6. 12 miles easy running
7. 12 miles easy running

Optimum Schedule

3rd Week

Day

1 15 miles easy running
2 20 × 440 in 82 — 220 R
3 9 miles easy running
4 5 × 880 in 2:45 — 440 R

5 7 miles easy running
6 8 × 330 in 50 — 550 R
7 15 miles easy running

4th Week

Day

1 12 miles easy running
2 12 × 220 in 39 — 220 R

3 8 miles easy running
4 1 mile in 5:20, ¾ mile in 4:00,
   880 in 2:30, 440 in 70 — all 440 R
5 9 miles easy running
6 6 miles with 6 × 120
   (fast and controlled)
7 15 miles easy running

Runner A

3rd Week*

Day

1 12 miles easy running
2 12 × 440 in 85 — 220 R
3 Rest day
4 5 × 880 in 2:45 — 440 R

5 7 miles easy running
6 3 miles easy running
7 Competition: 1-hour run (World
   Age Record), 10 miles 929 yards

4th Week

Day

1 12 miles easy running
2 12 × 220 in 39 — 220 R

3 8 miles easy running
4 1 mile in 5:20, ¾ mile in 4:00,
   880 in 2:30, 440 in 70 — all 440 R
5 9 miles easy running
6 6 miles with 6 × 120
   (fast and controlled)
7 15 miles easy running

Runner B

3rd Week

Day

1 9 miles in 63:00
2 A.M. 9 miles in 67:30
   P.M. 12 × 440 in 82 — 220 R
3 9 miles easy running
4 A.M. 2 × 2 miles in 11:45 —
   3-mile R
   P.M. 6 × 110 in 15 — 330 R
5 9 miles easy running
6 4 miles in 24:00
7 15 miles easy running

4th Week

Day

1 A.M. 12 miles easy running
   P.M. 8 × 440 in 82 — 220 R
2 A.M. 9 miles easy running
   P.M. 1 mile in 5:35, ¾ mile in
   4:06, 880 in 2:35, 440 in 66 — all
   440 R
3 9 miles easy running
4 A.M. 9 miles easy running
   P.M. 5 × 880 in 2:39 — 440 R
5 9 miles in 69:00
6 9 miles with 6 × 120
   (fast and controlled)
7 18 miles in 2:15:00

*Gradual resumption of normal 10K training.

Optimum Schedule	Runner A	Runner B
5th Week	*5th Week*	*5th Week*
Day	*Day*	*Day*
1 6 miles easy running, 3 miles in 17:00, 3 miles easy running	1 6 miles easy running, 3 miles in 17:00, 3 miles easy running	1 A.M. 10 miles in 70:00 / P.M. 4 miles in 24:00
2 12 × 220 in 36 — 220 R	2 12 × 220 in 36 — 220 R	2 16 × 220 in 37 — 220 R
3 7 miles easy running	3 7 miles easy running	3 9 miles easy running
4 4 × 1 mile in 5:40 — 660 R	4 4 × 1 mile in 5:40 — 660 R	4 A.M. 9 miles easy running / P.M. 4 × 1 mile in 5:27 — 880 R
5 Rest day	5 Rest day	5 9 miles easy running
6 6 miles easy running	6 6 miles easy running	6 9 miles easy running
7 10 miles in 58:00	7 8K race (U.S. Age Record) in 27:21	7 21 miles easy running
6th Week	*6th Week*	*6th Week*
Day	*Day*	*Day*
1 15 miles easy running	1 15 miles easy running	1 15 miles in 1:52:30
2 12 × 440 in 80 — 220 R	2 12 × 220 in 36 — 220 R	2 A.M. 8 miles easy running / P.M. 12 × 440 in 82 — 220 R
3 9 miles easy running	3 9 miles easy running	3 13 miles easy running
4 12 × 220 in 35 — 220 R	4 A.M. 6 miles easy running / P.M. 2 × 2 miles in 11:15 — 880 R	4 A.M. 6 miles easy running / P.M. 10 × 220 in 37 — 220 R
5 9 miles easy running	5 8 miles easy running with 6 × 110 (fast and controlled)	5 8 miles easy running
6 2 × 2 miles in 10:45 — 880 R	6 5 miles easy running	6 9 miles easy running
7 12 miles easy running	7 12 miles easy running	7 21 miles easy running

Mark

Allan

Optimum Schedule

7th Week
Day
1 12 miles easy running
2 16 × 110 in 16 — 330 R
3 9 miles easy running
4 2 × 1.5 miles in 8:00 — 880 R
5 Rest day
6 9 miles easy running
7 2 miles easy running, 10 miles in 57:30

8th Week
Day
1 12 miles easy running
2 8 × 440 in 85 — 220 R
3 2 × 2 miles in 11:40 — 660 R
4 6 miles easy running with 6 × 110 in 17
5 Rest day
6 3 miles easy jog
7 10K in 34:00

Runner A

7th Week
Day
1 12 miles easy running
2 16 × 110 in 16 — 330 R
3 9 miles easy running
4 2 × 1.5 miles in 8:00 — 880 R
5 Rest day
6 6 miles easy running
7 15K in 52:21 (U.S. Age Record)

8th Week
Day
1 12 miles easy running
2 8 × 440 in 85 — 220 R
3 2 × 2 miles in 11:40 — 660 R
4 6 miles easy running with 6 × 110 in 17
5 Rest day
6 3 miles easy jog
7 10K in 34:20 (U.S. Age Record)

Runner B

7th Week
Day
1 12 miles easy running
2 A.M. 12 miles easy running
P.M. 6 × 880 in 2:44 — 440 R
3 9 miles easy running
4 A.M. 7 miles easy running
P.M. 10 × 110 in 16 — 330 R
5 9 miles easy running
6 Rest day
7 20 miles with 5 miles in 28:09

8th Week
Day
1 12 miles easy running
2 10 × 440 in 78.5 — 220 R
3 13 miles with 3 miles in 18:00
4 4 × 220 in 36, 3 × 880 in 2:39, 4 × 220 in 36 — all 440 R
5 9 miles easy running
6 Rest day
7 10K in 33:51

As we said at the outset, the goal for both runners was a sub–34-minute 10K. All empirical experience indicated that Runner A should have attained this standard, and his final eight weeks of training and racing supported this view. Runner B, on the other hand, did not appear to have the necessary base to achieve his objective, even though his final eight weeks of training leading up to his attempt were eminently satisfactory. Runner A raced consistently during the final eight weeks, while Runner B had no racing during this period except for a 5-mile effort during a 20-mile training run.

Runner A was author Allan Lawrence (a fifty-two-year-old company executive) and runner B was author Mark Scheid, a thirty-six-year-old university professor.

There can only be speculation as to *why* Allan Lawrence fell a little short of his specific goal (perhaps too close to a marathon, or too much racing before the 10K attempt, or a combination of both combined with marginally tough training).

Mark Scheid approached his attempt obviously undertrained in the period prior to the final eight weeks — and appeared *underraced*. Yet Scheid was successful in his objective and Lawrence was a classic example of "almost, but not quite."

These examples demonstrate the occasional complexity of endurance racing and training and illustrate that even the best-laid plans can go awry (as was the case with Allan Lawrence's), and often surprising and unexpected performances (like Mark Scheid's) will occur. Self-coached runners will be better equipped to analyze these complexities when they can review a *written* schedule and a training diary and so be able to make reasonable assumptions as to "why" something did or did not take place. The bottom line is that often (but not too frequently) a realistic time objective will sometimes be unfulfilled. If the runner, however, has performed up to potential on any given day, there should be no regrets. There is always *another race, another chance,* to attempt the same goal.

The 36-Minute 10K

You are ready to train for a 36-minute 10K if you can run:

220 yards in 31 seconds
440 yards in 67 seconds
1 mile in 5 minutes 10 seconds

To run 10K in 36 minutes you need to average 5:49 per mile.

An eight-week base of 50 to 65 miles weekly is necessary before beginning the final eight weeks of 36-minute 10K training. A typical week should consist of:

- one long stamina run of 10 to 12 miles at 7:30 to 8:30 per mile
- two endurance workouts on the track (interval 220's, 440's, 880's, or single miles, all slightly faster than anticipated race pace)
- one medium-distance run (5 to 8 miles) with 4 to 8 strides of 60 to 130 yards at a fast and controlled pace
- three medium-distance (5 to 8 miles) maintenance runs at 7:30 to 8:30 per mile.

The athletes attempting to run 36 minutes for 10K are a husband-and-wife team who train and race together. Both have been running for two years before beginning a structured training program. Cynthia is a thirty-year-old mother and homemaker; Paul is a thirty-year-old oil field geologist.

"Easy running" in this schedule is 7:30 to 8:30 per mile.

1st Week

Day

1   10 miles easy running
2   440 in 80, 880 in 2:45; ¾ mile in 4:20, 1 mile in 5:55 — all 440 R*
3   6 miles easy running
4   4 miles in 25:00
5   9 miles easy running
6   9 miles easy running incorporating 5 × 220 (fast and controlled)
7   12 miles easy running

2nd Week

Day

1   12 miles easy running incorporating 2× 3 miles in 19:30
1   12 × 220 in 36 — 220 R
3   6 miles easy running
4   16 × 55 (fast and controlled) — 165 R
5   6 miles easy running
6   3 miles easy running
7   Competition: 8K in 29:20

*Run 440 yards in 80 seconds, 880 yards in 2 minutes 45 seconds, ¾ mile in 4 minutes 20 seconds, 1 mile in 5 minutes 55 seconds, with a 440-yard recovery in between.

3rd Week

Day

1 12 miles easy running
2 8 × 440 in 90 — 440 R
3 6 miles easy running
4 3 × 110 in 18 — 330 R; jog 440;
   2 miles in 12:00; jog 880; 2 ×
   440 in 80 — 220 R
5 6 miles easy running
6 3 miles easy running
7 ¼-marathon race: 38:54

4th Week

Day

1 12 miles easy running
2 12 × 220 in 40 — 440 R
3 7 miles easy running
4 2 × 2 miles in 12:00 — 880 R
5 9 miles easy running
6 6 miles easy running
7 15 miles easy running
   incorporating 9 miles in 58:30

5th Week

Day

1 12 miles easy running
2 8 × 220 in 38 — 440 R
3 6 miles easy running
4 4 × 220 in 38 — 220 R; jog 440;
   2 × 1 mile in 5:45 — 660 R; jog
   880; 2 × 220 in 35 — 220 R
5 Rest day
6 5 miles easy running
7 Competition at 10K OR time trial
   at 10K

6th Week

Day

1 12 miles easy running
2 8 × 220 in 38 — 440 R
3 10 miles in 70:00
4 4 × 330 in 60 — 110 R; jog 880;
   4 × 330 in 52 — 110 R
5 6 miles easy running
6 9 miles easy running
7 15 miles easy running

7th Week

Day

1 15 miles easy running
   incorporating 6 miles in 36:00
2 6 × 880 in 2:50 — 440 R
3 9 miles easy running
4 4 × 1 mile in 5:50 — 660 R
5 6 miles easy running
6 6 miles easy running
7 15 miles easy running

8th Week

Day

1 12 miles easy running
2 6 × 440 in 72 — 440 R
3 6 miles easy running
   incorporating 2 miles in 11:45
4 4 miles easy running
5 Rest day
6 4 miles easy running
7 Cajun Cup 10K race: 35 minutes
   10 seconds

The 38-Minute 10K

You are ready to train for a 38-minute 10K if you can run:

220 yards in 33 seconds
440 yards in 70 seconds
1 mile in 5 minutes 35 seconds

To run 10K in 38 minutes you need to average 6:08 per mile.

An eight-week base of 50 to 65 miles weekly is necessary before beginning the final eight-week 38-minute 10K training. A typical week should consist of:

- one long stamina run of 10 to 12 miles at 7:45 to 8:45 per mile
- one endurance workout on the track (interval 220's, 440's, 880's, or single miles, all slightly faster than anticipated race pace)
- one medium-distance run (5 to 8 miles) with 6 strides of 60 to 130 yards, run at a fast and controlled pace
- four medium-distance (5 to 8 miles) maintenance runs at 7:45 to 8:45 per mile.

The training histories below demonstrate two different approaches to training for this particular 10K goal by runners with diverse backgrounds and goals.

John is a thirty-year-old salesman who has been running recreationally for two years. He plans to use his increased ability at 10K as a stepping-stone to better marathon times. John will be following the "Optimum" schedule.

Kim is a thirty-year-old professional tennis player of international caliber. Initially he began a running program while recovering from shoulder surgery, but he now feels that his increased leg strength from running and his improved endurance enable him to "get to the ball quicker." Kim's weekly mileage has averaged only in the mid-twenties, but he has maintained a program of 6 to 10 strides of 40 to 60 yards at a fast and controlled pace in each workout. Kim is following a modified schedule tailored to fit around his tennis activities.

"Easy running" in both schedules is 7:45 to 8:45 per mile.

John — Optimum Schedule	Kim — Modified Schedule
1st Week	*1st Week*
Day	*Day*
1 10 miles easy running	1 Rest day
2 10 × 220 in 40 — 220 R*	2 A.M. 5 miles in 34:00
	P.M. 4 miles in 36:00
3 6 miles easy running	3 A.M. 5 miles in 34:00
	P.M. 4 miles in 36:00

*Run 220 yards in 40 seconds, 10 times, with a 220-yard recovery in between.

John — Optimum Schedule

1st Week (cont.)

Day

4 1 mile in 6:10, ¾ mile in 4:30, 880 in 2:55, 440 in 80, 220 in 35 — all 660 R

5 4 miles easy running

6 Rest day

7 12 miles easy running

2nd Week

Day

1 9 miles easy running incorporating 2 miles in 12:30

2 10 × 440 in 90 — 220 R

3 3 miles easy running

4 4 miles easy running incorporating 4 × 110 (fast and controlled)

5 5 miles easy running incorporating 1 mile in 5:32

6 3 miles easy running

7 15 miles easy running

3rd Week

Day

1 9 miles easy running

2 880 in 3:10; 440 in 88; 220 in 40; 110 in 18 — all 440 R; repeat set two times

3 7 miles easy running

4 3 × 1 mile in 6:20 — 880 R

5 10 miles easy running

6 3 miles easy running

7 15 miles easy running

Kim — Modified Schedule

1st Week (cont.)

Day

4 A.M. 5 miles in 34:00
   P.M. 10 × 440 in 75 — 220 R

5 A.M. 5 miles in 34:00
   P.M. 4 miles in 36:00

6 A.M. 4 miles easy running
   P.M. 10 × 440 in 75 — 220 R

7 Rest day

2nd Week

Day

1 A.M. 5 miles in 34:00
   P.M. 4 miles easy running

2 A.M. 5 miles in 34:00
   P.M. 3 × 880 in 3:00 — 220 R

3 A.M. 5 miles in 34:00
   P.M. 4 miles in 29:00

4 A.M. 5 miles in 34:00
   P.M. 8 × 440 in 72 — 220 R

5 A.M. 5 miles in 35:00
   P.M. 4 miles in 28:00

6 A.M. 5 miles easy running
   P.M. 10 × 440 in 75 — 220 R

7 Rest day

3rd Week

Day

1 Rest day

2 A.M. 5 miles in 35:00
   P.M. 4 miles in 30:00

3 A.M. 5 miles in 36:00
   P.M. 4 miles in 27:00

4 A.M. 5 miles in 34:00
   P.M. 8 × 440 in 70 — 220 R

5 A.M. 5 miles in 35:00
   P.M. 4 miles in 28:00

6 A.M. 5 miles easy running
   P.M. 10 × 440 in 75 — 220 R

7 Rest day

John — Optimum Schedule	Kim — Modified Schedule

John — Optimum Schedule

4th Week

Day

1 12 miles easy running incorporating 3 miles in 19:00

2 5 × 880 in 3:00 — 660 R

3 9 miles easy running

4 1 mile in 6:00; 880 in 2:52; 440 in 83 — all 660 R; jog 880; repeat set

5 9 miles easy running

6 Rest day

7 15 miles easy running

5th Week

Day

1 10 miles easy running incorporating 6 miles in 42:00

2 12 miles easy running

3 10 × 220 in 43 — 220 R

4 8 × 440 in 90 — 220 R

5 7 miles easy running

6 Rest day

7 8 miles easy running incorporating 5 miles in 31:00

6th Week

Day

1 12 miles easy running

2 10 × 220 in 40 — 440 R

3 9 miles easy running

Kim — Modified Schedule

4th Week

Day

1 Rest day

2 A.M. 6 miles easy running
   P.M. 4 miles in 27:00

3 A.M. 4 miles easy running
   P.M. 6 miles in 42:00

4 A.M. 6 miles easy running
   P.M. 12 × 220 in 33 — 220 R

5 A.M. 5 miles in 32:30
   P.M. 5 miles easy running

6 A.M. 6 miles easy running
   P.M. 6 × 440 in 68 — 220 R

7 Rest day

5th Week

Day

1 Rest day

2 A.M. 5 miles easy running
   P.M. 5 miles easy running

3 A.M. 4 miles in 28:00
   P.M. 6 miles easy running

4 A.M. 6 miles easy running
   P.M. 10 × 440 in 72 — 220 R

5 A.M. 4 miles in 26:00
   P.M. 6 miles in 42:00

6 A.M. 4 miles easy running
   P.M. 6 × 440 in 66 — 220 R

7 Rest day

6th Week

Day

1 A.M. 5 miles easy running
   P.M. 4 miles in 25:00

2 A.M. 6 miles easy running
   P.M. 4 miles in 28:00

3 A.M. 5 miles easy running
   P.M. 5 miles in 35:00

John — Optimum Schedule

6th Week (cont.)

Day

4   3 × 1 mile in 6:00 — 660 R

5   6 miles easy running
6   4 miles easy running

7   15 miles easy running

7th Week

Day

1   12 miles easy running
    incorporating 3 miles in 21:00
2   6 miles easy running

3   4 × 1 mile in 6:15 — 660 R
4   6 miles easy running

5   10 × 440 in 90 — 220 R
6   3 miles easy running

7   15 miles easy running
    incorporating 6 miles in 42:00

8th Week

Day

1   12 miles easy running
2   5 × 880 in 2:50 — 440 R
3   9 miles easy running
4   4 miles easy running
5   Rest day
6   6 miles easy running
7   10K race: 37 minutes 5 seconds

Kim — Modified Schedule

6th Week (cont.)

Day

4   A.M. 4 miles easy running
    P.M. 16 × 220 in 36 — 220 R
5   10 miles easy running
6   A.M. 4 miles easy running
    P.M. 10 × 440 in 72 — 220 R
7   Rest day

7th Week

Day

1   Rest day

2   A.M. 5 miles in 35:00
    P.M. 4 miles in 28:00
3   12 miles easy running
4   A.M. 4 miles in 28:00
    P.M. 10 × 440 in 70 — 220 R
5   8 miles in 56:00
6   A.M. 5 miles easy running
    P.M. 12 × 220 in 33 — 220 R
7   Rest day

8th Week

Day

1   Rest day
2   10 miles in 70:00
3   10 × 440 in 72 — 220 R
4   5 miles in 35:00
5   Rest day
6   4 miles easy running
7   10K race: 37 minutes 28 seconds

The 40-Minute 10K

> *You are ready to train for a 40-minute 10K if you can run:*
>
> 220 *yards in 36 seconds*
> 440 *yards in 75 seconds*
> 1 *mile in 5 minutes 45 seconds*
>
> *To run 10K in 40 minutes you need to average 6:28 per mile.*

The 40-minute 10K represents an important milestone for every aspiring distance runner, and is thought of by many as the border between merely being "respectable" and real competitive racing. It is particularly significant for women runners, as many local races can be won with times just under 40 minutes.

An eight-week base of 40 to 55 miles weekly is necessary before attempting the final eight-week 40-minute 10K training. A typical week's training should consist of:

- one long stamina run of 10 to 12 miles at 8:00 to 8:30 per mile
- one endurance workout on the track (interval 220's, 440's, 880's, or single miles, all slightly faster than anticipated race pace)
- one medium-distance run (5 to 8 miles) with 6 strides of 60 to 130 yards, run at a fast and controlled pace
- four medium-distance runs of 4 to 7 miles at 8:00 to 8:30 per mile.

Laurie, whose progress we will follow in the training below, is typical; she was an average recreational runner for two years before she decided to train more seriously for the 10K and ultimately the marathon. We pick up her schedule eight weeks before her first attempt to break 40 minutes.

"Easy running" in this schedule is 8:00 to 8:30 per mile.

1st Week	*2nd Week*
Day	*Day*
1 10 miles easy running	1 12 miles easy running
2 10 × 440 in 90 — 220 R*	2 12 × 220 in 40 — 220 R
3 6 miles easy running	3 6 miles easy running
4 12 × 110 in 17 — 330 R	4 16 × 55 (fast and controlled) – 385 R
5 6 miles easy running	5 6 miles easy running
6 7 miles easy running incorporating 3 miles in 22:00	6 8 miles easy running incorporating 4 miles in 28:00
7 10 miles easy running	7 12 miles easy running

*Run 440 yards in 90 seconds, 10 times, with a 220-yard recovery in between.

3rd Week

Day

1 12 miles easy running
   incorporating 2 miles in 12:00
2 6 miles easy running
3 3 × 220 in 40 — 220 R; jog 660;
   6 × 440 in 82 — 440 R; jog 660;
   3 × 220 in 40 — 220 R
4 5 miles easy running
5 7 miles easy running
   incorporating 5 miles in 35:00
6 Rest day
7 10 miles easy running

4th Week

Day

1 12 miles easy running
2 5 × 880 in 3:00 — 660 R
3 6 miles easy running
4 16 × 110 in 17 — 330 R
5 7 miles easy running
6 10 miles in 70:00
7 10 miles easy running

5th Week

Day

1 440 in 85, 880 in 3:00, 1 mile in
   6:10 — all 440 R; jog 880; 1 mile
   in 6:00, 880 in 2:50, 440 in 80 —
   all 440 R
2 9 miles easy running
3 6 miles easy running
   incorporating 4 × 130 (fast and
   controlled)
4 12 × 440 in 90 — 220 R
5 7 miles easy running
6 Rest day
7 5K race: 19:20

6th Week

Day

1 12 miles easy running
2 2 × 2 miles in 13:00 — 880 R
3 9 miles easy running
4 4 × 440 in 78 — 880 R
5 8 miles easy running
6 6 miles easy running
7 12 miles easy running

7th Week

Day

1 12 miles easy running
   incorporating 2 × 3 miles in 20:00
2 10 × 110 in 18 — 330 R
3 6 miles easy running
4 3 × 220 in 42 — 220 R; jog 880;
   2 × 880 in 3:00 — 440 R; jog
   880; 3 × 220 in 38 — 220 R
5 5 miles easy running
6 9 miles easy running
   incorporating 6 miles in 42:00
7 10 miles easy running

8th Week

Day

1 9 miles easy running
2 12 × 220 in 39 — 440 R
3 6 miles easy running
   incorporating 2 miles in 12:30
4 Rest day
5 6 miles easy running
6 3 miles easy running
7 10K race: 39 minutes 15 seconds

The 42-Minute 30-Second 10K

You are ready to train for a 42-minute 30-second 10K
if you can run:

220 yards in 37 seconds
440 yards in 78 seconds
1 mile in 5 minutes 55 seconds

To run 10K in 42 minutes 30 seconds you need to average
6:52 per mile.

An eight-week base of 30 to 45 miles weekly is recommended before beginning the final eight weeks of training for the 42-minute 30-second 10K. A typical week's training should consist of:

- one long stamina run of 10 miles at 8:15 to 8:45 per mile
- one endurance workout on the track (interval 220's, 440's, 880's, or single miles, all slightly faster than anticipated race pace)
- one medium-distance run (4 to 7 miles) with 6 strides of 60 to 130 yards, run at a fast and controlled pace
- four medium-distance runs of 3 to 6 miles at 8:15 to 8:45 per mile.

"Easy running" in this schedule is 8:15 to 8:45 per mile.

1st Week

Day

1 7 miles easy running
2 8 × 440 in 93 — 220 R*
3 6 miles easy running
4 6 × 110 in 19 — 330 R
5 6 miles easy running
6 Rest day OR 4 miles easy running
7 7 miles easy running
  incorporating 4 miles in 31:00

2nd Week

Day

1 9 miles easy running
2 10 × 220 in 42 — 220 R
3 5 miles easy running
4 12 × 55 (fast and controlled) —
  385 R
5 5 miles easy running
6 Rest day OR 4 miles easy running
7 7 miles easy running
  incorporating 5 miles in 38:45

*Run 440 yards in 93 seconds, 8 times, with a 220-yard recovery in between.

3rd Week

Day

1. 10 miles easy running
2. 440 in 88, 880 in 3:08, ¾ mile in 4:45, 1 mile in 6:30 — all 440 R
3. 6 miles easy running
4. 5 × 880 in 3:10 — 660 R
5. 5 miles easy running
6. Rest day OR 4 miles easy running
7. 6 miles easy running incorporating 5 miles in 38:45

4th Week

Day

1. 12 miles easy running
2. 10 × 440 in 90 — 220 R
3. 6 miles easy running
4. 12 × 110 in 20 — 330 R
5. 7 miles easy running
6. Rest day OR 4 miles easy running
7. Race: 5K to 15K OR 12 miles easy running incorporating 9 miles in 67:30

5th Week

Day

1. 9 miles easy running
2. 10 × 110 in 19 — 330 R
3. 7 miles easy running incorporating 2 × 1 mile in 6:20
4. 5 miles easy running
5. Rest day
6. 5 miles easy running
7. Race: 5K to 15K OR 4 miles in 27:30

6th Week

Day

1. 12 miles easy running
2. 3 × 1 mile in 6:25 — 660 R
3. 8 miles easy running
4. 10 × 440 in 84 — 220 R
5. 6 miles easy running incorporating 3 × 150 (fast and controlled)
6. 6 miles easy running
7. 6 miles easy running incorporating a 2-mile time trial OR 5K to 10K Race may be substituted

7th Week

Day

1. 10 miles easy running
2. 6 × 880 in 3:10 — 440 R
3. 6 miles easy running
4. 4 × 330 in 65 — 110 R; jog 880; 4 × 330 in 59 — 110 R
5. 5 miles easy running
6. Rest day
7. 10 miles easy running incorporating 8 miles in 58:40

8th Week

Day

1. 10 miles easy running
2. 6 × 440 in 85 — 440 R
3. 5 miles easy running incorporating 2 miles in 13:00
4. 3 miles easy running
5. Rest day
6. 3 miles easy running
7. 10K race: 42 minutes 30 seconds

The 45-Minute 10K

You are ready to train for a 45-minute 10K if you can run:

220 yards in 38 seconds
440 yards in 82 seconds
1 mile in 6 minutes 20 seconds

To run 10K in 45 minutes you need to average 7:16 per mile.

An eight-week base of 30 to 45 miles weekly is necessary before beginning the final eight weeks of pre-race specialized training. A typical week's training should consist of:

- one long stamina run of 10 miles at 8:15 to 9:00 per mile
- one endurance workout on the track (interval 220's, 440's, 880's, or single miles, all slightly faster than anticipated race pace)
- one medium-distance run (4 to 7 miles) with 6 strides of 60 to 130 yards, run at a fast and controlled pace
- four medium-distance runs of 3 to 6 miles at 8:15 to 9:00 per mile.

This particular training history demonstrates how a determined runner can overcome obstacles that would seem to preclude attainment of her goal. Lynn, a thirty-three-year-old financial trust consultant, has been running for five years with a disheartening series of injuries. Although she has not quite met the criteria for a 45-minute 10K, she has demonstrated the ability to "hang in" when things get tough. The left-hand schedule is the "ideal" or "optimum" schedule Lynn was attempting; on the right hand is the modified schedule Lynn in fact ran.

"Easy running" in both schedules is 8:15 to 9:00 per mile.

Optimum Schedule	Modified Schedule
1st Week	*1st Week*
Day	*Day*
1 7 miles easy running	1 7 miles easy running
2 8 × 440 in 98 — 220 R*	2 4 × 110 in 21 — 330 R; jog 880; 4 × 220 in 47 — 220 R
3 6 miles easy running	3 6 miles easy running
4 8 × 110 in 22 — 330 R	4 4 × 110 in 22 — 330 R; jog 880; 4 × 220 in 46 — 220 R

*Run 440 yards in 98 seconds, 8 times, with a 220-yard recovery in between.

Optimum Schedule	Modified Schedule

1st Week (cont.)

Day

5   5 miles easy running
6   4 miles easy running
7   6 miles easy running
    incorporating 3 miles in 24:00

2nd Week

Day

1   10 miles easy running
2   8 × 220 in 44 — 220 R
3   5 miles easy running
4   12 × 55 (fast and controlled) —
    385 R
5   6 miles easy running
6   Rest day OR 4 miles easy running
7   7 miles easy running
    incorporating 4 miles in 31:40

3rd Week

Day

1   9 miles easy running
2   440 in 90, 880 in 3:15, ¾ mile in
    4:55, 1 mile in 6:45 — all 440 R
3   6 miles easy running
4   5 × 880 in 3:25 — 660 R
5   5 miles easy running
6   Rest day
7   Competition: 5K to 15K OR 6
    miles easy running incorporating
    4 miles in 31:40

4th Week

Day

1   12 miles easy running
2   8 × 440 in 94 — 220 R

3   6 miles easy running
4   12 × 110 in 21 — 330 R
5   6 miles easy running
6   Rest day
7   Competition: 5K to 15K OR 8
    miles in 64:00

1st Week (cont.)

Day

5   5 miles easy running
6   10 miles in 85:00
7   13 miles easy running

2nd Week

Day

1   10 miles easy running
2   5 miles easy running
3   Ill — no running
4   3 miles easy running
5   6 miles easy running
6   6 miles easy running
7   7 miles easy running

3rd Week

Day

1   9 miles easy running
2   8 × 220 in 43 — 220 R

3   6 miles easy running
4   6 miles easy running
5   6 miles easy running
6   Rest day
7   9 miles easy running
    incorporating 3 miles in 23:00

4th Week

Day

1   12 miles easy running
2   4 × 110 in 20 — 330 R; jog 880;
    4 × 220 in 45 — 220 R
3   6 miles easy running
4   8 × 110 in 20 — 330 R
5   4 miles easy running
6   6 miles easy running
7   10 miles in 80:00

Optimum Schedule	Modified Schedule

5th Week

Day

	Optimum		Modified

5th Week

Day

1 9 miles easy running
   incorporating 2 miles in 13:30
2 10 × 110 in 21 — 330 R

3 7 miles easy running
   incorporating 2 × 1 mile in 6:40
4 5 miles easy running
5 Rest day

6 5 miles easy running
7 6 miles easy running
   incorporating 4 miles in 31:40

6th Week

Day

1 10 miles easy running
2 3 × 1 mile in 6:50 — 660 R
3 7 miles easy running
   incorporating 2 × 1 mile in 6:40
4 5 miles easy running

5 Rest day
6 5 miles easy running
7 Competition: 5K to 10K OR
   4 miles in 31:40

7th Week

Day

1 10 miles easy running
2 5 × 880 in 3:25 — 660 R
3 6 miles easy running
4 3 × 330 in 68 — 110 R; jog 880;
   3 × 330 in 65 — 110 R
5 6 miles easy running
6 Rest day
7 10 miles easy running
   incorporating 8 miles in 62:00

5th Week

Day

1 9 miles easy running
   incorporating 3 miles in 20:15
2 2 × 110 in 20 — 330 R; jog 880;
   4 × 440 in 93 — 440 R
3 Ill — no running

4 5 miles easy running
5 5 miles easy running
   incorporating 1 mile in 6:31
6 Rest day
7 7 miles easy running

6th Week

Day

1 10 miles easy running
2 Ill — no running
3 7 miles easy running

4 5 miles easy running
   incorporating 2 × 220 in 39
5 Rest day
6 5 miles easy running
7 6 miles easy running

7th Week

Day

1 10 miles easy running
2 6 miles easy running
3 6 miles easy running
4 6 miles easy running

5 6 miles easy running
6 Rest day
7 12 miles easy running
   incorporating 6 miles in 45:00

Optimum Schedule	Modified Schedule

8th Week

Day

1   10 miles easy running
2   6 × 440 in 88 — 440 R
3   5 miles easy running
     incorporating 2 miles in 13:30
4   3 miles easy running
5   Rest day
6   3 miles easy running
7   10K race: 45 minutes

8th Week

Day

1   10 miles easy running
2   6 × 440 in 95 — 220 R
3   5 miles easy running

4   4 × 110 in 21 — 330 R
5   Rest day
6   3 miles easy running
7   10K race: 44 minutes 56 seconds

The 47-Minute 30-Second 10K

You are ready to train for a 47-minute 30-second 10K
if you can run:

220 yards in 39 seconds
440 yards in 85 seconds
1 mile in 6 minutes 45 seconds

To run 10K in 47 minutes 30 seconds you need to average
7:40 per mile.

An eight-week base of 25 to 40 miles weekly is necessary before beginning the final eight weeks of specialized training leading to a 47-minute 30-second 10K. A typical week's training should consist of:

- one long stamina run of 7 to 10 miles at 8:30 to 9:15 per mile
- one endurance workout on the track (the subject in this example did in fact do *two* track workouts weekly, because of her commitment to shorter distance competition) consisting of intervals (220's, 440's, 880's, or single miles, all slightly faster than anticipated race pace)
- one medium-distance run (3 to 5 miles) with 6 strides of 60 to 130 yards, run at a fast and controlled pace
- three medium-distance runs (3 to 5 miles) at 8:30 to 9:15 per mile
- one rest day.

Our subject is Frances, a thirty-seven-year-old health spa executive. Frances began a running program at thirty-four and has completed two marathons (Hawaii and Boston) in 5 hours and 4 hours 16 minutes respectively. When Frances began working with us two years ago, we determined that her potential for personal achievement probably rested in shorter distance races and sprints. Accordingly, her preparation concentrated on that goal. (In 1981 and 1982 Frances placed in National Master's Championships at distances from 50 to 600 yards.) She had been on the recommended base program for six weeks before her attempt at a 10K personal record. (Her best 10K is 49:05.) We pick up Frances's training eight weeks from her scheduled attempt.

"Easy running" in this schedule is 8:30 to 9:15 per mile.

1st Week
Day

1 6 miles easy running
2 8 × 440 in 1:45 — 220 R*
3 6 miles easy running
4 6 × 110 in 18 — 330 R
5 5 miles easy running
6 Rest day
7 6 miles easy running
   incorporating 3 miles in 24:45

2nd Week
Day

1 9 miles easy running
2 8 × 220 in 49 — 220 R
3 5 miles easy running
4 12 × 55 (fast and controlled) —
   385 R
5 5 miles easy running
6 4 miles easy running
7 6 miles easy running
   incorporating 4 miles in 32:00

3rd Week
Day

1 10 miles easy running
2 440 in 98, 880 in 3:26, ¾ mile in
   5:20, 1 mile in 7:15 — all 440 R
3 6 miles easy running
4 5 × 880 in 3:40 — 660 R
5 5 miles easy running
6 3 miles easy running
7 6 miles easy running
   incorporating 4 miles in 32:00

4th Week
Day

1 12 miles easy running
2 8 × 440 in 1:40 — 440 R
3 6 miles easy running
4 12 × 110 in 20 — 330 R
5 7 miles easy running
6 Rest day
7 10 miles easy running
   incorporating 8 miles in 68:00

5th Week
Day

1 9 miles easy running
   incorporating 2 miles in 16:00
2 10 × 110 in 21 — 330 R
3 7 miles easy running
   incorporating 2 × 1 mile in 7:50
4 5 miles easy running
5 Rest day
6 5 miles easy running
7 4 miles in 30:40

6th Week
Day

1 9 miles easy running
2 3 × 1 mile in 7:40 — 660 R
3 7 miles easy running
4 10 × 440 in 1:45 — 220 R
5 6 miles easy running
   incorporating 3 × 150 (fast and
   controlled)
6 6 miles easy running
7 6 miles easy running
   incorporating 2 miles in 14:00

7th Week
Day

1 10 miles easy running
2 5 × 880 in 3:35 — 660 R
3 6 miles easy running
4 3 × 330 in 75 — 110 R; jog 880;
   3 × 330 in 68 — 110 R
5 5 miles easy running
6 Rest day
7 10 miles easy running
   incorporating 8 miles in 65:20

8th Week
Day

1 10 miles easy running
2 6 × 440 in 90 — 440 R
3 5 miles easy running
   incorporating 2 miles in 16:00
4 3 miles easy running
5 Rest day
6 3 miles easy running
7 10K race: 47 minutes 11 seconds

*Run 440 yards in 1 minute 45 seconds, 8 times, with a 220-yard recovery in between.

The 50-Minute 10K

You are ready to train for a 50-minute 10K if you can run:

220 yards in 41 seconds
440 yards in 87 seconds
1 mile in 7 minutes 15 seconds

To run 10K in 50 minutes you need to average 8:05 per mile.

A six-week base of 25 to 35 miles weekly is necessary before beginning the final eight weeks of specialized training leading to a 50-minute 10K. A typical week's training during this period should consist of:

* one long stamina run of 7 to 9 miles at 8:45 to 9:30 per mile
* one endurance workout on the track (interval 220's, 440's, 880's, or single miles, all slightly faster than anticipated race pace)
* one medium-distance run of 3 to 5 miles with 6 strides of 60 to 130 yards, run at a fast and controlled pace
* three medium distance runs of 3 to 5 miles at 8:45 to 9:30 per mile
* one rest day.

This training history is a good example of an increasingly common occurrence in distance running: older individuals who take up the sport and achieve noteworthy results. Barbara, a fifty-three-year-old homemaker, has been running for several months to lose weight and to gain general fitness. She completed two 10K fun runs (54:27 and 53:14) before beginning a structured workout schedule.

"Easy running" in this schedule is 8:45 to 9:30 per mile.

1st Week
Day

1 6 miles easy running
2 8 × 440 in 1:47 — 220 R*
3 5 miles easy running
4 10 × 110 in 23 — 330 R
5 5 miles easy running
6 Rest day
7 6 miles easy running
   incorporating 3 miles in 26:00

2nd Week
Day

1 9 miles easy running
2 6 × 220 in 47 — 220 R
3 5 miles easy running
4 10 × 55 (fast and controlled) — 385 R
5 6 miles easy running
6 Rest day
7 6 miles easy running
   incorporating 4 miles in 32:20

---

*Run 440 yards in 1 minute 47 seconds, 8 times, with a 220-yard recovery in between.

3rd Week

Day

1 9 miles easy running
2 440 in 1:40, 880 in 3:40, ¾ mile in 5:40, 1 mile in 7:45 — all 440 R
3 6 miles easy running
4 5 × 880 in 3:50 — 660 R
5 5 miles easy running
6 3 miles easy running
7 6 miles easy running incorporating 4 miles in 32:20

4th Week

Day

1 12 miles easy running
2 8 × 440 in 1:45 — 440 R
3 6 miles easy running
4 12 × 110 in 22 — 330 R
5 7 miles easy running
6 Rest day
7 10 miles easy running incorporating 7 miles in 61:15

5th Week

Day

1 9 miles easy running incorporating 2 miles in 16:30
2 3 × 1 mile in 8:05 — 660 R
3 5 miles easy running
4 10 × 440 in 1:47 — 220 R
5 6 miles easy running
6 4 miles easy running incorporating 3 × 150 (fast and controlled)
7 6 miles easy running incorporating 2 miles in 15:40

6th Week

Day

1 5 miles easy running
2 3 × 880 in 3:40 — 880 R
3 7 miles easy running
4 6 × 440 in 92 — 660 R
5 6 miles easy running
6 Rest day
7 10 miles easy running

7th Week

Day

1 9 miles easy running
2 5 × 880 in 3:50 — 660 R
3 6 miles easy running
4 3 × 330 in 77 — 110 R; jog 880; 3 × 330 in 72 — 110 R
5 5 miles easy running
6 Rest day
7 10 miles easy running incorporating 8 miles in 70:00

8th Week

Day

1 9 miles easy running
2 6 × 440 in 95 — 440 R
3 5 miles easy running incorporating 2 miles in 16:30
4 3 miles easy running
5 Rest day
6 3 miles easy running
7 10K race: 50 minutes 3 seconds

The 52-Minute 30-Second 10K

> *You are ready to train for a 52-minute 30-second 10K*
> *if you can run:*
>
> *220 yards in 42 seconds*
> *440 yards in 89 seconds*
> *1 mile in 7 minutes 40 seconds*
>
> *To run 10K in 52 minutes 30 seconds you need to average*
> *8:20 per mile.*

A six-week base of 25 to 35 miles weekly is necessary before beginning the final eight weeks of specialized training leading to a 52-minute 30-second 10K. A typical week's training during this period should consist of:

- one long stamina run of 7 to 9 miles at 9:15 to 10:00 per mile
- one endurance workout on the track (interval 220's, 440's, 880's, or single miles, all slightly faster than anticipated race pace)
- one medium-distance run of 4 miles with 6 strides of 60 to 130 yards, run at a fast and controlled pace
- three medium-distance runs of 4 miles at 9:15 to 10:00 per mile
- one rest day.

The runner attempting to run 10K in 52 minutes 30 seconds is a forty-nine-year-old homemaker who completed the "survival" marathon preparation and finished the Boston Marathon in 4 hours 26 minutes 18 seconds. Janie followed the "recovery" program after Boston and then began her eight-week 10K program four weeks after her marathon debut.

"Easy running" in this schedule is 9:15 to 10:00 per mile.

1st Week	*2nd Week*
Day	*Day*
1 6 miles easy running	1 9 miles easy running
2 8 × 440 in 1:50 — 220 R*	2 8 × 220 in 51 — 220 R
3 3 miles easy running	3 5 miles easy running
4 8 × 110 in 23 — 330 R	4 12 × 55 (fast and controlled) — 385R
5 3 miles easy running	5 4 miles easy running
6 Rest day	6 3 miles easy running
7 6 miles easy running incorporating 3 miles in 27:00	7 6 miles easy running incorporating 4 miles in 34:00

*Run 440 yards in 1 minute 50 seconds, 8 times, with a 220-yard recovery in between.

3rd Week

Day

1. 9 miles easy running
2. 440 in 1:42, 880 in 3:50, ¾ mile in 5:50, 1 mile in 8:10 — all 440 R
3. 6 miles easy running
4. 5 × 880 in 4:05 — 660 R
5. 5 miles easy running
6. Rest day
7. 6 miles easy running incorporating 4 miles in 34:00

4th Week

Day

1. 10 miles easy running
2. 8 × 440 in 1:47 — 440 R
3. 6 miles easy running
4. 12 × 110 in 24 — 330 R
5. 2 miles easy running
6. 9 miles easy running
7. 3 miles easy running

5th Week

Day

1. 5-mile race: 42:02
2. 6 miles easy running
3. 6 miles easy running incorporating 2 × 1 mile in 8:20
4. 5 miles easy running
5. Rest day
6. 5 miles easy running
7. 6 miles easy running incorporating 2 miles in 16:10

6th Week

Day

1. 9 miles easy running
2. 3 × 1 mile in 8:20 — 660 R
3. 6 miles easy running
4. 10 × 440 in 1:50 — 220 R
5. 5 miles easy running incorporating 3 × 150 (fast and controlled)
6. 6 miles easy running
7. 6 miles easy running incorporating 4 miles in 33:30

7th Week

Day

1. 9 miles easy running
2. 4 × 880 in 3:55 — 660 R
3. 6 miles easy running
4. 3 × 330 in 79 — 110 R; jog 880; 3 × 330 in 74 — 110 R
5. 5 miles easy running
6. Rest day
7. 10 miles easy running incorporating 8 miles in 70:00

8th Week

Day

1. 9 miles easy running
2. 6 × 440 in 97 — 440 R
3. 5 miles easy running incorporating 2 miles in 17:00
4. 3 miles easy running
5. Rest day
6. 3 miles easy running
7. 10K race: 52 minutes 15 seconds

The 55-Minute 10K

A 55-minute 10K is attainable if you can run:

220 yards in 43 seconds
440 yards in 91 seconds
1 mile in 8 minutes

To run 10K in 55 minutes you need to average 8:54 per mile.

A six-week base of 20 to 30 miles weekly is recommended before beginning specialized training for the 55-minute 10K. A typical week's training should consist of:

- one long stamina run of 7 to 9 miles at 9:30 to 10:30 per mile
- one endurance workout on the track (interval 220's, 440's, 880's, or single miles, all slightly faster than anticipated race pace)
- one medium-distance run of 3 miles with 6 strides of 60 to 130 yards, run at a fast and controlled pace
- three medium-distance runs of 3 miles at 9:30 to 10:30 per mile
- one rest day.

"Easy running" in this schedule is 9:30 to 10:30 per mile.

1st Week

Day

1 6 miles easy running
2 8 × 440 in 1:55 — 220 R*
3 6 miles easy running
4 6–10 × 110 in 25 — 330 R
5 5 miles easy running
6 Rest day
7 6 miles easy running
   incorporating 3 miles in 28:00

2nd Week

Day

1 9 miles easy running
2 8 × 220 in 52 — 220 R
3 5 miles easy running
4 12 × 55 (fast and controlled) —
   385 R
5 5 miles easy running
6 Rest day
7 6 miles easy running
   incorporating 4 miles in 36:00

*Run 440 yards in 1 minute 55 seconds, 8 times, with a 220-yard recovery in between.

3rd Week

Day

1 9 miles easy running
2 440 in 1:44, 880 in 4:05, ¾ mile in 6:10, 1 mile in 8:20 — all 440 R
3 6 miles easy running
4 4 × 880 in 4:15 — 880 R
5 5 miles easy running
6 Rest day OR 2 miles easy running
7 6 miles easy running incorporating 4 miles in 35:30

4th Week

Day

1 9 miles easy running
2 8 × 440 in 1:50 — 440 R
3 6 miles easy running
4 12 × 110 in 25 — 330 R
5 6 miles easy running
6 Rest day OR 2 miles easy running
7 Race: 5K to 15K OR 7 miles in 65:20

5th Week

Day

1 8 miles easy running incorporating 2 miles in 17:45
2 8 × 110 in 24 — 330 R
3 6 miles easy running incorporating 2 × 1 mile in 8:50
4 5 miles easy running
5 Rest day
6 4 miles easy running
7 Race: 5K to 15K OR 6 miles easy running incorporating a 2-mile time trial

6th Week

Day

1 8 miles easy running
2 3 × 1 mile in 8:55 — 660 R
3 6 miles easy running
4 8 × 440 in 1:50 — 440 R
5 6 miles easy running incorporating 4 × 110 (fast and controlled)
6 5 miles easy running
7 6 miles easy running incorporating 4 miles in 35:30

7th Week

Day

1 8 miles easy running
2 4 × 880 in 4:08 — 660 R
3 6 miles easy running
4 3 × 330 in 80 — 110 R; jog 880; 3 × 330 in 75 — 110 R
5 5 miles easy running
6 Rest day
7 9 miles easy running incorporating 7 miles in 64:45

8th Week

Day

1 8 miles easy running
2 5 × 440 in 98 — 440 R
3 5 miles easy running incorporating 1.5 miles in 13:30
4 2 miles easy running
5 Rest day
6 2 miles easy running
7 10K race: 55 minutes

The Intermediate Long Distances

Fifteen Kilometers
10 Miles
1-Hour Run
Twenty Kilometers
½-Marathon

"I must a dozen mile tonight."
—HENRY IV, PART 2

For the self-coached runner who has begun her career as a recreational runner and then progressed to an "addicted" racer in runs up to the 10K distance, there will probably come a time when her fancy will turn to longer distances. While many runners find there is no problem converting from 10K training to marathon training, there is a growing percentage of runners who are now looking for intermediate-distance (15K, 10 miles, 1-hour run, 20K, and ½-marathon) races with the accompanying graduated training that will condition and prepare them for the ultimate challenge: the marathon.

The purpose of this chapter is to provide the necessary step that will allow the self-coached runner to advance with a regulated rate of training and racing from the 10K to the intermediate longer distances before attempting the marathon.

The following schedules have been designed and tested for the 10-mile distance, but times have also been indicated that are attainable for the 15K, 20K, and ½-marathon distances as spin-offs from the 10-mile schedule.

To choose the correct schedule the runner needs only to check the appropriate 10K time indicated for the individual 10-mile schedule. The foundation or base work for any of the 10-mile schedules should be an eight- to ten-week period of *pre-10K* training (see the schedules for 10K earlier in the chapter) and two to four weeks of *specific* 10K training before embarking on the appropriate 10-mile schedule.

After completing the 10-mile schedule, the runner may now proceed directly to the appropriate marathon schedule (see the schedules for the marathon later in the chapter).

It should be stressed again that the intermediate schedules are not absolutely necessary before a runner can attempt a marathon, but are deemed advisable only if the individual feels the need and is more comfortable with the concept and the practice of increasing racing training in incremental steps. They are also useful, of course, if a runner wishes to train specifically for races at these distances.

The 50-Minute 10 Miles

A 50-minute 10 miles is attainable if you can run:

10K in 30 minutes

To run 10 miles in 50 minutes you need to average 5:00 per mile.

Other intermediate-distance times that result from this 10-mile training are:

- 15K in 46 minutes (4:56 per mile average)
- 20K in 63 minutes 15 seconds (5:06 per mile average)
- ½-marathon in 67 minutes (5:07 per mile average).

"Easy running" in this schedule is 6:00 to 7:00 per mile.

1st Week

Day

1 15 miles easy running
2 3 × 2 miles in 10:30 — 880 R*
3 10 miles easy running
4 10 × 880 in 2:30 — 440 R
5 12 miles easy running
6 8 miles easy running
7 12 miles in 66:00

2nd Week

Day

1 18 miles easy running
2 12 × 440 in 68 — 440 R
3 10 miles easy running
4 5 × 1 mile in 5:10 — 440 R
5 25 × 110 in 17 — 110 R
6 10 miles easy running
7 2 × 6 miles in 34:00 — 1 mile R

3rd Week

Day

1 18 miles easy running
2 2 × 3 miles in 15:30 — 880 R
3 16 × 440 in 70 — 440 R
4 12 miles easy running
5 20 × 110 in 15 — 110 R
6 8 miles easy running
7 15 miles easy running

4th Week

Day

1 20 miles easy running
2 5 × 1-mile in 5:00 — 660 R
3 9 miles easy running
4 2 × 3 miles in 16:00 — 660 R
5 10 miles easy running
6 6 miles easy running
7 10 miles in 53:00

*Run 2 miles in 10 minutes 30 seconds, 3 times, with an 880-yard recovery in between.

5th Week

Day

1   12 miles easy running
2   16 × 440 in 68 — 220 R
3   12 miles easy running
4   440 in 72, 880 in 2:30, ¾ mile in 3:50, 1 mile in 5:10 — all 440 R; jog 880; 1 mile in 5:00, ¾ mile in 3:40, 880 in 2:20, 440 in 63 — all 440 R
5   10 miles easy running
6   8 miles easy running
7   6 miles in 30:00

6th Week

Day

1   20 miles easy running
2   25 × 110 in 16 — 330 R
3   10 miles easy running
4   6 × 880 in 2:15 — 660 R
5   Rest day
6   6 miles easy running
7   Competitive effort: 8K to 15K

7th Week

Day

1   12 miles easy running
2   10 × 440 in 80 — 440 R
3   10 miles easy running
4   2 × 1.5 miles in 7:15 — 880 R
5   6 miles easy running
6   Rest day
7   15 miles in 1 hour 30 minutes

8th Week

Day

1   12 miles easy running
2   6 × 880 in 2:30 — 440 R
3   6 miles easy running
4   3 × 1 mile in 5:00 — 660 R
5   Rest day
6   3 miles easy running
7   10 miles in 50 minutes

The 55-Minute 10 Miles

A 55-minute 10 miles is attainable if you can run:

10K in 33 minutes

To run 10 miles in 55 minutes you need to average 5:30 per mile.

Other intermediate-distance times that result from this 10-mile training are:

- 15K in 52 minutes (5:28 per mile average)
- 20K in 70 minutes 30 seconds (5:40 per mile average)
- ½-marathon in 74 minutes 30 seconds (5:41 per mile average).

"Easy running" in this schedule is 7:00 to 7:30 per mile.

1st Week

Day

1 15 miles easy running
2 3 × 2 miles in 11:00 — 880 R*
3 10 miles easy running
4 8 × 880 in 2:40 — 440 R
5 10 miles easy running
6 6 miles easy running
7 12 miles in 72:00

2nd Week

Day

1 18 miles easy running
2 10 × 440 in 70 — 440 R
3 10 miles easy running
4 5 × 1 mile in 5:20 — 440 R
5 20 × 220 in 38 — 220 R
6 10 miles easy running
7 2 × 5 miles in 29:00 — 1 mile R

3rd Week

Day

1 18 miles easy running
2 10 miles easy running
3 20 × 440 in 80 — 220 R
4 12 miles easy running
5 25 × 110 in 17 — 110 R
6 6 miles easy running
7 12 miles easy running

4th Week

Day

1 18 miles easy running
2 440 in 72, 880 in 2:35, ¾ mile in 4:00, 1 mile in 5:20 — all 440 R; jog 880; 1 mile in 5:10, ¾ mile in 3:50, 880 in 2:25, 440 in 68 — all 440 R
3 10 miles easy running
4 2 × 3 miles in 17:00 — 880 R
5 10 miles easy running
6 6 miles easy running
7 10 miles in 57:30

*Run 2 miles in 11 minutes, 3 times, with an 880-yard recovery in between.

5th Week

Day

1 15 miles easy running
2 20 × 440 in 80 — 220 R
3 12 miles easy running
4 4 × 1 mile in 5:20 — 440 R
5 10 miles easy running
6 6 miles easy running
7 3 × 2 miles in 10:45 — 880 R

6th Week

Day

1 20 miles easy running
2 8 × 440 in 66 — 440 R
3 9 miles easy running
4 4 × ¾ mile in 3:50 — 660 R
5 Rest day
6 6 miles easy running
7 Time trial or competitive effort at 10K

7th Week

Day

1 15 miles easy running
2 12 × 220 in 35 — 440 R
3 10 miles easy running
4 2 × 1.5 miles in 7:40 — 880 R
5 6 miles easy running
6 Rest day
7 18 miles easy running

8th Week

Day

1 12 miles easy running
2 6 × 880 in 2:40 — 440 R
3 6 miles easy running
4 2 × 2 miles in 11:30 — 660 R
5 Rest day
6 5 miles easy running
7 10 miles in 55 minutes

The 60-Minute 10 Miles

> *A 60-minute 10 miles is attainable if you can run:*
>
> *10K in 35 minutes 30 seconds*
>
> *To run 10 miles in 60 minutes you need to average 6:00 per mile.*

Other intermediate-distance times that result from this 10-mile training are:

- 15K in 54 minutes 50 seconds (5:54 per mile average)
- 20K in 76 minutes 30 seconds (6:09 per mile average)
- ½-marathon in 81 minutes (6:10 per mile average).

"Easy running" in this schedule is 7:30 to 8:15 per mile.

1st Week

Day

1 15 miles easy running
2 2 × 2 miles in 12:30 — 880 R*
3 10 miles easy running
4 6 × 880 in 2:50 — 660 R
5 10 miles easy running
6 8 miles easy running
7 10 miles in 68:00

2nd Week

Day

1 15 miles easy running
2 10 miles easy running
3 16 × 110 in 17 — 330 R
4 4 × 1 mile in 5:50 — 440 R
5 10 miles easy running
6 6 miles easy running
7 2 × 3 miles in 18:00 — 1 mile R

3rd Week

Day

1 18 miles easy running
2 6 miles easy running
3 20 × 440 in 85 — 220 R
4 10 miles easy running
5 3 × 1 mile in 5:45 — 440 R
6 7 miles easy running
7 10 miles easy running

4th Week

Day

1 15 miles easy running
2 20 × 220 in 40 — 220 R
3 10 miles easy running
4 2 × 3 miles in 18:30 — 880 R
5 10 miles easy running
6 3 miles easy running
7 10 miles in 65:00

*Run 2 miles in 12 minutes 30 seconds, 2 times, with an 880-yard recovery in between.

5th Week

Day

1 15 miles easy running
2 20 × 110 in 19 — 110 R
3 10 miles easy running
4 12 × 440 in 78 — 440 R
5 8 miles easy running
6 6 miles easy running
7 3 × 2 miles in 12:15 — 880 R

6th Week

Day

1 20 miles easy running
2 6 × 440 in 72 — 660 R
3 6 miles easy running
4 3 × 1 mile in 5:30 — 660 R
5 Rest day
6 3 miles easy running
7 Competitive effort OR time trial at 10K

7th Week

Day

1 12 miles easy running
2 10 × 220 in 40 — 440 R
3 9 miles easy running
4 2 × 1.5 miles in 8:40 — 880 R
5 6 miles easy running
6 Rest day
7 15 miles easy running

8th Week

Day

1 12 miles easy running
2 10 × 440 in 85 — 220 R
3 6 miles easy running
4 2 × 2 miles in 12:30 — 660 R
5 Rest day
6 3 miles easy running
7 10 miles in 60 minutes

The 65-Minute 10 Miles

A 65-minute 10 miles is attainable if you can run:

10K in 38 minutes 15 seconds

To run 10 miles in 65 minutes you need to average 6:30 per mile.

Other intermediate-distance times that result from this 10-mile training are:

- 15K in 59 minutes (6:24 per mile average)
- 20K in 83 minutes (6:42 per mile average)
- ½-marathon in 88 minutes 30 seconds (6:45 per mile average).

"Easy running" in this schedule is 7:45 to 8:45 per mile.

1st Week
Day

1   12 miles easy running
2   2 × 2 miles in 13:30 — 880 R*
3   9 miles easy running
4   6 × 880 in 3:05 — 660 R
5   9 miles easy running
6   6 miles easy running
7   10 miles in 72:00

2nd Week
Day

1   12 miles easy running
2   9 miles easy running
3   16 × 110 in 19 — 330 R
4   9 miles easy running
5   4 × 1 mile in 6:15 — 660 R
6   5 miles easy running
7   15 miles easy running

3rd Week
Day

1   2 × 3 miles in 21:00 — 1 mile R
2   6 miles easy running
3   16 × 440 in 90 — 220 R
4   10 miles easy running
5   Rest day
6   7 miles easy running
7   12 miles easy running

4th Week
Day

1   15 miles easy running
2   16 × 220 in 40 — 220 R
3   9 miles easy running
4   2 × 3 miles in 20:00 — 1 mile R
5   6 miles easy running
6   4 miles easy running
7   10 miles in 70:00

*Run 2 miles in 13 minutes 30 seconds, 2 times, with an 880-yard recovery in between.

5th Week

Day

1   12 miles easy running
2   16 × 110 in 19 — 330 R
3   9 miles easy running
4   8 × 440 in 82 — 440 R
5   9 miles easy running
6   3 miles easy running
7   12 miles in 84:00

6th Week

Day

1   15 miles easy running
2   12 × 110 in 19 — 110 R
3   3 miles easy running
4   3 × 1 mile in 6:00 — 440 R
5   Rest day
6   3 miles easy running
7   Competitive effort OR time trial at 10K

7th Week

Day

1   12 miles easy running
2   8 × 440 in 90 — 440 R
3   9 miles easy running
4   2 × 1.5 miles in 9:30 — 880 R
5   6 miles easy running
6   Rest day
7   12 miles easy running

8th Week

Day

1   10 miles easy running
2   10 × 220 in 40 — 220 R
3   6 miles easy running
4   2 × 2 miles in 13:30 — 660 R
5   Rest day
6   3 miles easy running
7   10 miles in 65 minutes

The 70-Minute 10 Miles

A 70-minute 10 miles is attainable if you can run:

10K in 42 minutes

To run 10 miles in 70 minutes you need to average 7:00 per mile.

Other intermediate-distance times that result from this 10-mile training are:

- 15K in 64 minutes 15 seconds (6:54 per mile average)
- 20K in 89 minutes 5 seconds (7:11 per mile average)
- ½-marathon in 95 minutes (7:15 per mile average).

"Easy running" in this schedule is 8:00 to 9:00 per mile.

1st Week

Day

1. 12 miles easy running
2. 2 × 2 miles in 14:30 — 880 R*
3. 8 miles easy running
4. 6 × 880 in 3:15 — 660 R
5. 7 miles easy running
6. 5 miles easy running
7. 10 miles in 77:30

2nd Week

Day

1. 12 miles easy running
2. 7 miles easy running
3. 16 × 110 in 20 — 330 R
4. 7 miles easy running
5. 4 × 1 mile in 6:45 — 660 R
6. 5 miles easy running
7. 15 miles easy running

3rd Week

Day

1. 2 × 3 miles in 21:30 — 1 mile R
2. 6 miles easy running
3. 3 × 1 mile in 6:30 — 440 R
4. 9 miles easy running
5. Rest day
6. 7 miles easy running
7. 12 miles easy running

4th Week

Day

1. 12 miles easy running
2. 16 × 220 in 42 — 220 R
3. 9 miles easy running
4. 3 × 2 miles in 14:00 — 1 mile R
5. 6 miles easy running
6. Rest day
7. 10 miles in 75:00

---

*Run 2 miles in 14 minutes 30 seconds, 2 times, with an 880-yard recovery in between.

5th Week

Day

1 12 miles easy running
2 10 × 220 in 40 — 220 R
3 9 miles easy running
4 2 × 3 miles in 21:00 — 1 mile R
5 6 miles easy running
6 3 miles easy running
7 12 miles in 90:00

6th Week

Day

1 13 miles easy running
2 12 × 110 in 20 — 110 R
3 3 miles easy running
4 3 × 1 mile in 6:30 — 440 R
5 Rest day
6 3 miles easy running
7 Competitive effort OR time trial at 10K

7th Week

Day

1 12 miles easy running
2 8 × 440 in 94 — 440 R
3 8 miles easy running
4 2 × 1.5 miles in 10:10 — 880 R
5 6 miles easy running
6 Rest day
7 10 miles easy running

8th Week

Day

1 10 miles easy running
2 10 × 220 in 42 — 220 R
3 6 miles easy running
4 2 × 1 mile in 6:00 — 1 mile R
5 Rest day
6 3 miles easy running
7 10 miles in 70 minutes

The 75-Minute 10 Miles

A 75-minute 10 miles is attainable if you can run:

10K in 43 minutes 45 seconds

To run 10 miles in 75 minutes you need to average 7:30 per mile.

Other intermediate-distance times that result from this 10-mile training are:

- 15K in 67 minutes 30 seconds (7:22 per mile average)
- 20K in 95 minutes 30 seconds (7:42 per mile average)
- ½-marathon in 102 minutes (7:46 per mile average).

"Easy running" in this schedule is 8:15 to 9:15 per mile.

1st Week

Day

1 12 miles easy running
2 2 × 2 miles in 15:30 — 880 R*
3 7 miles easy running
4 6 × 880 in 3:30 — 660 R
5 6 miles easy running
6 5 miles easy running
7 10 miles in 80:00

2nd Week

Day

1 10 miles easy running
2 6 miles easy running
3 16 × 110 in 21 — 330 R
4 6 miles easy running
5 4 × 1 mile in 7:15 — 660 R
6 6 miles easy running
7 13 miles easy running

3rd Week

Day

1 2 miles easy running, 6 miles in 46:00, 3 miles easy running
2 6 miles easy running
3 3 × 1 mile in 7:00 — 440 R
4 7 miles easy running
5 Rest day
6 6 miles easy running
7 15 miles easy running

4th Week

Day

1 10 miles in 80:00
2 16 × 110 in 20 — 330 R
3 7 miles easy running
4 3 × 2 miles in 15:00 — 1 mile R
5 Rest day
6 6 miles easy running
7 3 miles easy running, 5 miles in 37:30, 2 miles easy running

*Run 2 miles in 15 minutes 30 seconds, 2 times, with an 880-yard recovery in between.

5th Week

Day

1 10 miles easy running
2 10 × 220 in 44 — 220 R
3 7 miles easy running
4 2 × 3 miles in 23:30 — 1 mile R
5 6 miles easy running
6 3 miles easy running
7 12 miles in 95:00

6th Week

Day

1 10 miles easy running
2 8 × 220 in 42 — 440 R
3 4 miles easy running
4 4 × 880 in 3:10 — 660 R
5 Rest day
6 3 miles easy running
7 2 miles easy running, 6 miles in 45:00, 2 miles easy running

7th Week

Day

1 10 miles easy running
2 8 × 440 in 98 — 440 R
3 7 miles easy running
4 2 × 1.5 miles in 10:30 — 880 R
5 Rest day
6 6 miles easy running
7 9 miles easy running

8th Week

Day

1 4 miles easy running, 4 miles in 30:00, 2 miles easy running
2 6 × 440 in 1:45 — 440 R
3 5 miles easy running
4 2 × 1 mile in 7:00 — 1 mile R
5 Rest day
6 3 miles easy running
7 10 miles in 75 minutes

The 80-Minute 10 Miles

> *An 80-minute 10 miles is attainable if you can run:*
>
> *10K in 46 minutes 20 seconds*
>
> *To run 10 miles in 80 minutes you need to average 8:00 per mile.*

Other intermediate-distance times that result from this 10-mile training are:

- 15K in 73 minutes (7:50 per mile average)
- 20K in 102 minutes 20 seconds (8:15 per mile average)
- ½-marathon in 109 minutes 15 seconds (8:20 per mile average).

"Easy running" in this schedule is 8:45 to 9:30 per mile.

1st Week

Day

1 12 miles easy running
2 2 × 2 miles in 16:30 — 880 R*
3 6 miles easy running
4 5 × 880 in 3:45 — 660 R
5 6 miles easy running
6 3 miles easy running
7 10 miles in 85:00

2nd Week

Day

1 10 miles easy running
2 6 miles easy running
3 16 × 110 in 22 — 330 R
4 6 miles easy running
5 3 × 1 mile in 7:30 — 660 R
6 6 miles easy running
7 12 miles easy running

3rd Week

Day

1 2 miles easy running, 6 miles in 50:00, 2 miles easy running
2 6 miles easy running
3 3 × 1 mile in 7:30 — 440 R
4 6 miles easy running
5 Rest day
6 6 miles easy running
7 15 miles easy running

4th Week

Day

1 10 miles in 85:00
2 12 × 110 in 20 — 330 R
3 6 miles easy running
4 2 × 2 miles in 16:00 — 1 mile R
5 6 miles easy running
6 Rest day
7 3 miles easy running, 5 miles in 40:00, 2 miles easy running

*Run 2 miles in 16 minutes 30 seconds, 2 times, with an 880-yard recovery in between.

5th Week

Day

1 9 miles easy running
2 8 × 220 in 46 — 220 R
3 6 miles easy running
4 2 × 3 miles in 24:00 — 1 mile R
5 6 miles easy running
6 2 miles easy running
7 12 miles in 1:42:00

6th Week

Day

1 9 miles easy running
2 12 × 110 in 20 — 110 R
3 4 miles easy running
4 4 × 880 in 3:35 — 660 R
5 Rest day
6 3 miles easy running
7 2 miles easy running, 6 miles in 48:00, 2 miles easy running

7th Week

Day

1 10 miles easy running
2 8 × 440 in 1:40 — 440 R
3 6 miles easy running
4 2 × 1.5 miles in 11:30 — 880 R
5 Rest day
6 5 miles easy running
7 8 miles easy running

8th Week

Day

1 4 miles easy running, 4 miles in 32:00, 2 miles easy running
2 6 miles easy running
3 4 × 1 mile in 7:45 — 880 R
4 4 miles easy running
5 Rest day
6 3 miles easy running
7 10 miles in 80 minutes

The 85-Minute 10 Miles

An 85-minute 10 miles is attainable if you can run:

10K in 49 minutes

To run 10 miles in 85 minutes you need to average 8:30 per mile.

Other intermediate-distance times that result from this 10-mile training are:

- 15K in 77 minutes 30 seconds (8:18 per mile average)
- 20K in 108 minutes 30 seconds (8:45 per mile average)
- ½-marathon in 116 minutes (8:50 per mile average).

"Easy running" in this schedule is 9:00 to 10:00 per mile.

1st Week

Day

1 10 miles easy running
2 12 × 110 in 24 — 330 R*
3 6 miles easy running
4 5 × 880 in 4:00 — 660 R
5 6 miles easy running
6 3 miles easy running
7 10 miles in 90:00

2nd Week

Day

1 6 miles easy running
2 2 × 2 miles in 17:30 — 880 R
3 6 miles easy running
4 3 × 1 mile in 8:00 — 660 R
5 6 miles easy running
6 Rest day
7 12 miles easy running

3rd Week

Day

1 2 miles easy running, 6 miles in 52:00, 2 miles easy running
2 6 miles easy running
3 3 × 1 mile in 8:00 — 440 R
4 6 miles easy running
5 Rest day
6 4 miles easy running
7 13 miles easy running

4th Week

Day

1 10 miles in 90:00
2 12 × 110 in 22 — 330 R
3 5 miles easy running
4 2 × 2 miles in 17:00 — 1 mile R
5 Rest day
6 3 miles easy running
7 3 miles easy running, 5 miles in 42:30, 2 miles easy running

*Run 110 yards in 24 seconds, 12 times, with a 330-yard recovery in between.

5th Week

Day

1   6 miles easy running
2   8 × 220 in 50 — 220 R
3   5 miles easy running
4   2 × 3 miles in 25:30 — 1 mile R
5   6 miles easy running
6   3 miles easy running
7   10 miles in 87:30

6th Week

Day

1   9 miles easy running
2   12 × 110 in 22 — 110 R
3   4 miles easy running
4   4 × 880 in 3:45 — 660 R
5   Rest day
6   3 miles easy running
7   2 miles easy running, 6 miles in 51:00, 2 miles easy running

7th Week

Day

1   10 miles easy running
2   6 miles easy running
3   4 × 1 mile in 8:00 — 880 R
4   3 miles easy running
5   Rest day
6   3 miles easy running
7   6 miles easy running

8th Week

Day

1   4 miles easy running, 4 miles in 34:00, 2 miles easy running
2   5 miles easy running
3   3 × 1 mile in 8:00 — 880 R
4   3 miles easy running
5   Rest day
6   3 miles easy running
7   10 miles in 85 minutes

The 90-Minute 10 Miles

A 90-minute 10 miles is attainable if you can run:

10K in 52 minutes

To run 10 miles in 90 minutes you need to average 9:00 per mile.

Other intermediate-distance times that result from this 10-mile training are:

- 15K in 82 minutes (8:48 per mile average)
- 20K in 115 minutes (9:15 per mile average)
- ½-marathon in 122 minutes 15 seconds (9:20 per mile average).

"Easy running" in this schedule is 9:45 to 10:30 per mile.

1st Week

Day

1 10 miles easy running
2 8 × 220 in 52 — 220 R*
3 6 miles easy running
4 3 × 880 in 4:15 — 880 R
5 4 miles easy running
6 Rest day
7 10 miles in 97:30

2nd Week

Day

1 6 miles easy running
2 10 × 110 in 24 — 330 R
3 4 miles easy running
4 2 × 1 mile in 8:45 — 880 R
5 3 miles easy running
6 Rest day
7 12 miles easy running

3rd Week

Day

1 1 mile easy running, 5 miles in 47:30, 1 mile easy running
2 4 miles easy running
3 2 × 1 mile in 8:30 — 880 R
4 5 miles easy running
5 Rest day
6 6 miles easy running
7 13 miles easy running

4th Week

Day

1 6 miles easy running
2 8 × 440 in 2:00 — 440 R
3 5 miles easy running
4 2 × 2 miles in 18:00 — 1 mile R
5 3 miles easy running
6 3 miles easy running
7 2 miles easy running, 5 miles in 45:00, 2 miles easy running

*Run 220 yards in 52 seconds, 8 times, with a 220-yard recovery in between.

5th Week

Day

1 6 miles easy running
2 8 × 220 in 52 — 220 R
3 5 miles easy running
4 2 × 3 miles in 28:30 — 1 mile R
5 6 miles easy running
6 Rest day
7 12 miles easy running

6th Week

Day

1 9 miles easy running
2 12 × 110 in 24 — 110 R
3 4 miles easy running
4 3 × 880 in 4:00 — 880 R
5 Rest day
6 3 miles easy running
7 2 miles easy running, 6 miles in 54:00, 1 mile easy running

7th Week

Day

1 10 miles easy running
2 6 miles easy running
3 3 × 1 mile in 8:30 — 880 R
4 4 miles easy running
5 Rest day
6 3 miles easy running
7 5 miles easy running

8th Week

Day

1 3 miles easy running, 4 miles in 36:00, 1 mile easy running
2 4 miles easy running
3 3 × 1 mile in 8:30 — 660 R
4 3 miles easy running
5 Rest day
6 3 miles easy running
7 10 miles in 90 minutes

The Marathon

"Alas! The way is wearisome and long!"
—Two Gentlemen of Verona

The 2-Hour 20-Minute Marathon

> *A 2-hour 20-minute marathon is attainable if you can run:*
>
> *1 mile in 4 minutes 20 seconds*
> *10K in 30 minutes 30 seconds*
>
> *To run a 2-hour 20-minute marathon you need to average*
> *5:20 per mile.*

A ten-week base of 75 to 95 miles weekly is necessary before you begin the final ten-week schedule leading to a 2-hour 20-minute marathon. A typical training week during this period should include:

- one long stamina run of 16 to 20 miles at 6:30 to 7:00 per mile
- two endurance workouts on the track, each consisting of one of the following:
  - 20 × 110 yards in 16 seconds, with a 330-yard recovery in between
  - 16 × 440 yards in 72 seconds, with a 440-yard recovery in between
  - 8 × 880 yards in 2 minutes 30 seconds, with a 440-yard recovery in between
  - 6 × ¾ mile in 3 minutes 50 seconds, with a 660-yard recovery in between
  - 4 × 1 mile in 5 minutes 10 seconds, with an 880-yard recovery in between
- three days of easy running (12 to 15 miles) at 6:30 to 7:00 per mile
- one 6 to 10 miles controlled pace run at 5:20 per mile.

Like the 30-minute 10K, the 2-hour 20-minute marathon belongs to a steadily growing elite group of endurance runners. The 2-hour 20-minute marathon standard has not yet been achieved by women — although the super-elite distance-running females are slowly edging down toward this barrier. The key, I feel, for women to reach and surpass 2 hours 20 minutes in the marathon will be in their ability to first lower their times for 10K. Only then will they have the necessary requisites of speed and endurance to maintain a 5:20 per mile pace for the distance. As of this writing, only about a dozen women in the world have surpassed 4:20 for the mile, while no woman has run 10K in less than 31 minutes.

Our subject for the 2-hour 20-minute marathon is David, a twenty-seven-year-old sports store manager. David exemplifies the characteristics of dedication, discipline, and motivation that all runners at this level must possess. David's previous best marathon on a certified course is 2 hours 23 minutes 12 seconds.

"Easy running" in this schedule is 6:00 to 6:45 per mile.

1st Week

Day

1   15 miles easy running
2   12 × 440 in 75 — 110 R*
3   10 miles easy running
4   12 miles incorporating 10 miles in 54:00
5   12 miles easy running
6   6 miles easy running
7   18 miles in 1:48:00

2nd Week

Day

1   15 miles easy running
2   30 × 110 in 17 — 110 R
3   8 miles easy running
4   10 × 440 in 67 — 440 R
5   12 miles easy running
6   10 miles easy running
7   20 miles in 2:00:00

3rd Week

Day

1   15 miles easy running
2   6 × 1 mile in 5:10 — 440 R
3   10 miles easy running
4   16 × 220 in 34 — 220 R
5   6 miles easy running
6   6 miles easy running
7   25K race: 1:19:30

4th Week

Day

1   12 miles easy running
2   6 miles easy running
3   16 × 110 in 16 — 110 R
4   12 × 440 in 70 — 440 R
5   10 miles easy running
6   8 miles easy running
7   22 miles easy running

5th Week

Day

1   15 miles easy running
2   4 × 1 mile in 5:00 — 440 R
3   12 miles easy running
4   2 × 2 miles in 9:40 — 880 R
5   10 miles easy running
6   6 miles easy running
7   15 miles in 1:20:00

6th Week

Day

1   20 miles easy running
2   12 miles easy running
    incorporating 3 miles in 14:30
3   Rest day
4   12 miles easy running
5   4 × 660 in 1:36 — 660 R
6   Rest day
7   30K race: 1:33:50

* Run 440 yards in 75 seconds, 12 times, with a 110-yard recovery in between.

7th Week

Day

1   12 miles easy running
2   6 miles easy running
3   9 miles easy running
4   3 × 2 miles in 10:30 — 880 R
5   10 miles easy running
6   10 miles in 57:30
7   15 miles easy running

8th Week

Day

1   10 miles easy running
2   20 miles easy running
3   12 miles incorporating 2 × 2 miles in 10:00
4   20 × 440 in 72 — 220 R
5   10 miles easy running
6   6 miles easy running
7   24 miles in 2:33:00

9th Week

Day

1   15 miles easy running
2   12 miles incorporating 3 miles in 15:00
3   20 × 110 in 19 — 110 R
4   12 miles easy running
5   12 miles incorporating 10 miles in 54:00
6   6 miles easy running
7   15 miles in 1:30:00

10th Week

Day

1   12 miles easy running
2   Rest day
3   9 miles easy running
4   3 × 1 mile in 5:10 — 660 R
5   Rest day
6   8 miles easy running
7   Rest day

11th Week

Day

1   Houston-Tenneco Marathon
    2 hours 17 minutes 13 seconds

The 2-Hour 30-Minute Marathon

A 2-hour 30-minute marathon is attainable if you can run:

1 mile in 4 minutes 40 seconds
10K in 32 minutes 30 seconds

To run a 2-hour 30-minute marathon you need to average 5:43 per mile.

A ten-week base of 75 to 90 miles weekly is necessary before you begin the final ten weeks of specialized training leading to a 2-hour 30-minute marathon. A typical training week during this period should include:

- one long stamina run of 14 to 19 miles at 6:45 to 7:30 per mile
- two endurance workouts on the track, each consisting of one of the following:
  - 6 to 8 × 880 yards in 2 minutes 40 seconds, with an 880-yard recovery in between
  - 5 × ¾ mile in 4 minutes, with an 880-yard recovery in between
  - 3 × 1 mile in 5 minutes 35 seconds, with an 880-yard recovery in between
  - 16 × 440 yards in 78 seconds, with a 440-yard recovery in between
- four days of easy running (9 to 12 miles) at 6:45 to 7:30 per mile.

In this case history we will follow the progress of Tad, a twenty-six-year-old printing-shop proprietor who has been running for six years distances from 5K to the marathon. Tad originally attended college on a basketball scholarship, but three operations resulting in the surgical removal of cartilage and ligaments from his left knee forced his premature retirement from that sport and the beginning of a career as an endurance runner. (Tad is somewhat limited in the degree of knee flexibility because of his surgery, but has compensated by developing powerful upper and lower leg strength through physical therapy and weight work.) Tad's fastest marathon before his attempt below is 2 hours 38 minutes 24 seconds.

"Easy running" in this schedule is 6:45 to 7:30 per mile.

1st Week

Day

1 18 miles easy running
2 10 × 440 in 76 — 110 R*
3 12 miles easy running
   incorporating 10 miles in 60:00
4 3 × 1 mile in 5:15 — 440 R
5 Rest day
6 6 miles easy running
7 ½-marathon race: 1:12:00

2nd Week

Day

1 12 miles easy running
2 12 × 220 in 38 — 220 R
3 9 miles easy running
   incorporating 3 miles in 17:00
4 6 × 880 in 2:30 — 660 R
5 10 miles easy running
6 Rest day
7 20K race: 1:07:30

3rd Week

Day

1 10 miles easy running
2 10 × 110 in 16 — 330 R
3 ¾ mile in 3:36, 880 in 2:20, 440
   in 66, 220 in 30 — all 660 R
4 10 miles easy running
5 12 miles easy running
6 10 miles easy running
7 15 miles easy running
   incorporating 2 × 3 miles in 17:00

4th Week

Day

1 18 miles easy running
2 16 × 440 in 82 — 220 R
3 12 miles easy running
   incorporating 6 miles in 36:00
4 4 × 220 in 38 — 220 R; jog 440;
   4 × 440 in 70 — 440 R; jog 440;
   4 × 220 in 35 — 220 R
5 Rest day
6 6 miles easy running
7 10-mile race: 53:40

5th Week

Day

1 15 miles easy running
2 12 × 220 in 39 — 110 R
3 10 miles easy running
4 6 × 880 in 2:40 — 220 R
5 6 miles easy running
6 10 miles easy running
7 21 miles in 2:16:30

6th Week

Day

1 15 miles easy running
   incorporating 2 × 1 mile in 5:15
2 8 × 220 in 32 — 440 R
3 6 miles easy running
4 3 × 220 in 39 — 220 R; 2 × 1
   mile in 5:30 — 660 R; 3 × 220 in
   34 — 220 R
5 Rest day
6 6 miles easy running
7 10 miles easy running
   incorporating 10K in 32:30

* Run 440 yards in 76 seconds, 10 times, with a 110-yard recovery in between.

7th Week

Day

1 15 miles easy running
2 10 × 440 in 85 — 440 R
3 10 miles easy running
4 9 miles easy running
   incorporating 6 miles in 34:30
5 Rest day
6 5 miles easy running
7 25K race: 1:25:29

8th Week

Day

1 15 miles easy running
2 10 × 440 in 85 — 440 R
3 10 miles easy running
4 2 × 2 miles in 11:20 — 880 R
5 12 miles easy running
6 12 miles easy running
7 23 miles easy running

9th Week

Day

1 15 miles easy running
2 8 × 880 in 2:52 — 660 R
3 6 miles easy running
4 12 × 440 in 78 — 220 R
5 21 miles in 2:09:30
6 12 miles easy running
7 15 miles in 1:30:00

10th Week

Day

1 12 miles easy running
2 6 miles easy running
3 Rest day
4 10 × 220 in 40 — 220 R
5 Rest day
6 45 minutes easy running
7 Dallas White Rock Marathon
   2 hours 29 minutes 10 seconds

The 2-Hour 40-Minute Marathon

A 2-hour 40-minute marathon is attainable if you can run:

1 mile in 5 minutes
10K in 34 minutes 30 seconds

To run a 2-hour 40-minute marathon you need to average
6:06 per mile.

A ten-week base of 70 to 90 miles weekly is recommended before you begin the final ten weeks of specialized training leading to a 2-hour 40-minute marathon. Included in a typical week's training during this phase should be:

- one long stamina run of 14 to 18 miles at 7:30 to 8:00 per mile
- one medium-long endurance run of 8 to 12 miles at 6:45 to 7:30 per mile
- two endurance workouts on the track, each consisting of one of the following:
  - 16 × 440 yards in 85 seconds, with a 440-yard recovery in between
  - 6 to 8 × 880 yards in 2 minutes 50 seconds to 3 minutes, with an 880-yard recovery in between
  - 4 × ¾ mile in 4 minutes 20 seconds to 4 minutes 30 seconds, with an 880-yard recovery in between
  - 3 × 1 mile in 5 minutes 50 seconds to 6 minutes, with an 880-yard recovery in between
- three days of easy running with 4 to 8 × 80 to 130 yards at a fast and controlled pace.

The following schedule is a chronicle of author Lawrence's attempt to return to top running form and achieve the personal goal of running 2:40 in the 1983 Houston-Tenneco Marathon. This attempt was made nine months after major surgery, and this training was closely monitored by co-author Scheid for an impersonal analysis of training progress.

We pick up Lawrence's preparation ten weeks from the set goal.

"Easy running" in this schedule is 7:30 to 8:00 per mile.

1st Week

Day

1. 18 miles easy running
2. 10 × 440 in 80 — 220 R*
3. 12 miles easy running
   incorporating 10 miles in 65:00
4. 3 × 1 mile in 5:45 — 440 R
5. Rest day
6. 6 miles easy running
7. ½-marathon race: 1:19:02

2nd Week

Day

1. 12 miles easy running
2. 12 × 220 in 38 — 440 R
3. 10 miles easy running
4. 6 × 880 in 2:45 — 660 R
5. 9 miles easy running
6. 3 miles easy running
7. 15 miles easy running
   incorporating 12 miles in 72:00

3rd Week

Day

1. 15 miles easy running
2. 10 × 110 in 17 — 330 R
3. 10 miles easy running
4. Rest day
5. 6 miles easy running
6. 4 miles easy running
7. Dallas White Rock Marathon
   2 hours 41 minutes 44 seconds**

4th Week

Day

1. 4 miles easy running
2. 4 miles easy running
3. Rest day
4. Rest day
5. Rest day
6. Rest day
7. 10 miles easy running

5th Week

Day

1. 10 miles easy running
2. 4 × 880 in 3:00 — 880 R
3. 12 miles easy running
4. 6 miles easy running
   incorporating 2 miles in 12:00
5. 9 miles easy running
6. 3 miles easy running
7. 18 miles easy running

6th Week

Day

1. 12 miles easy running
   incorporating 2 × 1 mile in 5:30
2. 6 × 880 in 2:45 — 440 R
3. 6 miles easy running
4. 9 miles easy running
   incorporating 6 miles in 36:00
5. 9 miles easy running
6. 5 miles easy running
7. 21 miles in 2:21:45

* Run 440 yards in 80 seconds, 10 times, with a 220-yard recovery in between.

** The Dallas White Rock Marathon was to be a 20-mile training run at 6:30 per mile, but good running conditions plus the author's occasional bouts of "impulsiveness" saw him running faster than scheduled and farther than the distance intended.

7th Week

Day

1 15 miles easy running
2 10 × 440 in 85 — 440 R
3 6 miles easy running
4 10 miles easy running
   incorporating 6 miles in 36:00
5 Rest day
6 5 miles easy running
7 15 miles in 1:29:00

8th Week

Day

1 18 miles easy running
2 3 × 1 mile in 5:40 — 220 R
3 10 miles easy running
4 2 × 2 miles in 11:45 — 880 R
5 12 miles easy running
6 6 miles easy running
7 21 miles in 2:23:30

9th Week

Day

1 15 miles easy running
2 16 × 440 in 82 — 220 R
3 6 miles easy running
4 5 × 880 in 2:45 — 220 R
5 18 miles in 2:01:30
6 Rest day
7 12 miles easy running
   incorporating 10 miles in 58:00

10th Week

Day

1 12 miles easy running
2 6 miles easy running
3 2 × 2 miles in 12:00 — 660 R
4 Rest day
5 5 miles easy running
6 Rest day
7 5 miles easy running

11th Week

Day

1 Houston-Tenneco Marathon
   2 hours 39 minutes 59 seconds

The 2-Hour 50-Minute Marathon

A 2-hour 50-minute marathon is attainable if you can run:

1 mile in 5 minutes 15 seconds
10K in 36 minutes 45 seconds

To run a 2-hour 50-minute marathon you need to average
6:29 per mile.

A ten-week base of 70 to 80 miles weekly is necessary before you begin the final ten-week countdown before the 2-hour 50-minute marathon goal. A typical week's training during the initial ten-week base period should include:

- one long stamina run of 12 to 18 miles at 7:30 to 8:30 per mile
- two track workouts with the emphasis on short to medium aerobic training, each consisting of one of the following:
  - 12 × 220 yards in 39 seconds, with a 220-yard to 440-yard recovery in between
  - 10 to 16 × 440 yards in 88 seconds, with a 440-yard recovery in between
  - 4 to 6 × 880 yards in 2 minutes 52 seconds to 3 minutes, with an 880-yard recovery in between
- four days of easy running (7 to 10 miles) at 7:30 to 8:30 per mile.

Our subject for the attempt to run a marathon in 2 hours 50 minutes is Vanessa, a twenty-nine-year-old pharmacist. Vanessa has been running for three years and her best marathon has been 2 hours 53 minutes 10 seconds before the attempt described below. During the base, or foundation, period, Vanessa has raced three times at distances ranging from 5K to 10K.

For this particular schedule we provide the "ideal" training along with what Vanessa actually ran.

"Easy running" in both schedules is 7:30 to 8:30 per mile.

Optimum Schedule	Vanessa

1st Week

Optimum Schedule

Day

1 15 miles easy running
2 12 × 220 in 39 — 220 R*
3 9 miles easy running
4 12 miles easy running
5 3 × 1 mile in 6:00 — 880 R
6 3 miles easy running
7 12 miles easy running
   incorporating 10 miles in 65:00

Vanessa

Day

1 15 miles easy running
2 12 × 220 in 39 — 220 R*
3 12 miles easy running
4 12 miles easy running
5 Rest day
6 3 miles easy running
7 15K race: 56:10

2nd Week

Optimum Schedule

Day

1 15 miles easy running
2 10 miles easy running
3 18 miles easy running
   incorporating 2 miles in 12:00
4 6 miles easy running
5 Rest day
6 6 miles easy running
7 Competition: 10 miles plus OR 15
   miles at marathon pace (6:29)

Vanessa

Day

1 12 miles easy running
2 10 miles easy running
3 18 miles easy running
   incorporating 2 miles in 12:00
4 6 miles easy running
5 Rest day
6 6 miles easy running
7 25K race: 1:39:40

3rd Week

Optimum Schedule

Day

1 10 miles easy running
2 8 miles easy running
3 3 × 1 mile in 5:50 — 880 R
4 10 miles easy running
   incorporating 2 × 1 mile in 6:00
5 Rest day
6 6 miles easy running
7 20 miles easy running

Vanessa

Day

1 15 miles easy running
2 8 miles easy running
3 Rest day
4 10 miles easy running
   incorporating 2 × 1 mile in 6:00
5 Rest day
6 6 miles easy running
7 23 miles easy running

4th Week

Optimum Schedule

Day

1 12 miles easy running
2 12 miles easy running
   incorporating 6 × 110 in 19 (fast
   and controlled)
3 12 × 440 in 85 — 440 R
4 12 miles easy running

Vanessa

Day

1 12 miles easy running
2 12 miles easy running
   incorporating 6 × 110 in 19 (fast
   and controlled)
3 12 × 440 in 88 — 440 R
4 12 miles easy running

*Run 220 yards in 39 seconds, 12 times, with a 220-yard recovery in between.

Optimum Schedule	Vanessa

4th Week (cont.)

Day

5 10 miles easy running
6 6 miles in 39:00
7 10 miles easy running
   incorporating 6 miles in 37:30

5th Week

Day

1 20 miles easy running

2 15 miles easy running
3 4 × 1 mile in 5:45 — 660 R
4 10 miles easy running
   incorporating 4 × 220 (fast and
   controlled)
5 5 miles easy running
6 Rest day
7 Competition: 15K to 25K OR 15
   miles at marathon pace (6:29)

6th Week

Day

1 10 miles easy running
2 12 miles easy running
3 6 × 880 in 3:00 — 660 R
4 2 × 2 miles in 11:45 — 880 R
5 12 miles easy running

6 9 miles easy running
7 21 miles easy running

7th Week

Day

1 12 miles easy running
2 12 × 440 in 90 — 220 R
3 8 miles easy running
4 6 miles easy running
5 4 × 1 mile in 6:00 — 440 R
6 9 miles easy running
7 18 miles in 1:57:00

4th Week (cont.)

Day

5 10 miles easy running
6 6 miles in 39:00
7 10 miles easy running

5th Week

Day

1 18 miles easy running
   incorporating 6 miles in 38:00
2 15 miles easy running
3 4 × 1 mile in 5:45 — 660 R
4 10 miles easy running
   incorporating 4 × 220 (fast and
   controlled)
5 5 miles easy running
6 Rest day
7 ½-marathon race: 1:24:05

6th Week

Day

1 10 miles easy running
2 12 miles easy running
3 12 miles easy running
4 2 × 2 miles in 11:45 — 880 R
5 12 miles easy running
   incorporating 2 × 1 mile in 5:40
6 9 miles easy running
7 21 miles easy running

7th Week

Day

1 12 miles easy running
2 12 × 440 in 90 — 220 R
3 8 miles easy running
4 6 miles easy running
5 Rest day
6 3 miles easy running
7 30K race: 1:57:04

Optimum Schedule	Vanessa

8th Week

Day

1	9 miles easy running
2	12 miles easy running
3	3 × 1.5 miles in 9:00 — 880 R
4	10 miles in 70:00
5	Rest day
6	8 miles easy running
7	18 miles in 2:06:00

9th Week

Day

1	17 miles easy running
2	8 × 440 in 85 — 220 R
3	3 × 2 miles in 12:00 — 880 R
4	12 miles easy running
5	10 miles easy running incorporating 3 × 1 mile in 5:45
6	10 miles easy running
7	10K race OR 6 miles in 37:00

10th Week

Day

1	10 miles easy running
2	Rest day
3	8 miles easy running
4	Rest day
5	6 miles easy running
6	Rest day
7	Marathon in 2 hours 50 minutes

8th Week

Day

1	9 miles easy running
2	12 miles easy running
3	15 miles easy running
4	10 miles in 70:00
5	Rest day
6	8 miles easy running
7	20 miles in 2:15:00

9th Week

Day

1	17 miles easy running
2	8 × 440 in 85 — 220 R
3	3 × 2 miles in 12:00 — 880 R
4	12 miles easy running
5	15 miles easy running incorporating 9 miles in 60:00
6	10 miles easy running
7	12 miles easy running

10th Week

Day

1	10 miles easy running
2	Rest day
3	8 miles easy running
4	Rest day
5	6 miles easy running
6	Rest day
7	Houston-Tenneco Marathon 2 hours 44 minutes 44 seconds

It should be noted that several unusual circumstances assisted Vanessa's effort in this particular marathon schedule:

- Her job allowed her to train before she went to work at mid-morning; she was thus able to do excellent distance work in good running conditions without the tiredness caused by constant standing during her working hours.

- She was able to choose races that slowly built her distance-racing conditioning and psychologically prepared her for the marathon distance.
- She had a sound background of competitive experience in other sports (swimming, tennis, and basketball) that very nicely bolstered her competitive attitude toward endurance running.
- Professionally and personally it was a very good year for Vanessa.
- Vanessa was experiencing a dramatic breakthrough in the "coming up" process.

The 3:00 Marathon

The development of the 3-hour marathoner is discussed in Chapter 2. See pages 27–33.

The 3-Hour 10-Minute Marathon

A 3-hour 10-minute marathon is attainable if you can run:

1 mile in 5 minutes 50 seconds
10K in 41 minutes

*To run a 3-hour 10-minute marathon you need to average
7:14 per mile.*

A ten-week base of 45 to 60 miles weekly is necessary before you begin the final ten weeks of specialized training leading to the 3-hour 10-minute marathon. A typical week's training during this period should consist of:

- one long stamina run of 12 to 15 miles at 8:00 to 9:00 per mile
- two track workouts, each consisting of one of the following:
  - 10 × 440 yards in 88 seconds, with a 440-yard recovery in between
  - 4 to 6 × 880 yards in 3 minutes 5 seconds to 3 minutes 15 seconds, with an 880-yard recovery in between
  - 4 × ¾ mile in 4 minutes 45 seconds, with an 880-yard recovery in between
  - 3 × 1 mile in 6 minutes 20 seconds, with an 880-yard recovery in between
- four days of easy running (6 to 10 miles) at 8:00 to 9:00 per mile.

Our case history subject is a forty-one-year-old homemaker who began running at age thirty-six after the birth of her first child. Her fastest marathon before the one recorded below was 3 hours 12 minutes 46 seconds. Mary has also competed with distinction in the Master's Division in national competition in distances from 5K to 30K — winning or placing in many instances — and has completed one ultra-marathon of 50 miles.

"Easy running" in this schedule is 8:00 to 9:00 per mile.

1st Week

Day

1 8 miles easy running
2 8 miles easy running
   incorporating 5 × 150 (fast and
   controlled)
3 8 miles easy running
   incorporating 6 miles in 45:00
4 10 miles easy running
5 1 mile in 6:30, ¾ mile in 4:40,
   880 in 3:06, 3 × 220 in 40 — all
   440 R*
6 5 miles easy running
7 12 miles easy running

2nd Week

Day

1 8 miles easy running
2 8 × 440 in 95 — 440 R
3 6 miles easy running
4 8 miles easy running
   incorporating 5 × 220 in 39
5 Rest day
6 3 miles easy running
7 10K race: 42:26

3rd Week

Day

1 10 miles easy running
2 3 miles easy running
3 8 miles easy running
4 6 × 440 in 90 — 220 R
5 10 miles easy running
6 Rest day
7 12 miles easy running

4th Week

Day

1 12 miles easy running
2 8 × 220 in 40 — 220 R
3 10 miles easy running
   incorporating 6 miles in 42:00
4 6 miles easy running
5 6 × 880 in 3:10 — 440 R
6 6 miles easy running
7 18 miles easy running

5th Week

Day

1 15 miles easy running
2 Rest day
3 10 miles in 70:00
4 3 × 1 mile in 6:45 — 440 R
5 6 miles easy running
6 4 miles easy running
7 30K race: 2:10:06

6th Week

Day

1 3 miles easy running
2 6 miles easy running
3 12 miles easy running
   incorporating 6 × 110 (fast and
   controlled)
4 6 miles easy running
5 3 miles in 21:00 — 1 mile R; 4 ×
   220 in 40 — 220 R
6 10 miles easy running
7 18 miles easy running

*Run 1 mile in 6 minutes 30 seconds, ¾ mile in 4 minutes 40 seconds, 880 yards in 3 minutes 6 seconds, 220 yards in 40 seconds 3 times, with a 440-yard recovery between all efforts.

7th Week

Day

1   18 miles easy running
2   9 miles easy running
    incorporating 6 × 110 (fast and
    controlled)
3   10 miles in 70:00
4   Rest day
5   15 miles easy running
6   5 × 1 mile in 6:30 — 440 R
7   10 miles easy running

8th Week

Day

1   21 miles easy running
2   10 miles easy running
    incorporating 3 miles in 19:30
3   Rest day
4   6 miles in 42:00
5   15 miles easy running
6   12 miles easy running
7   15 miles in 1:48:45

9th Week

Day

1   12 miles easy running
2   Rest day
3   3 × 220 in 40 — 220 R; jog 880;
    2 miles in 13:00
4   10 miles easy running
5   18 miles easy running
6   12 miles easy running
7   10 miles in 70:00

10th Week

Day

1   Rest day
2   6 miles easy running
3   6 miles easy running
4   3 miles easy running
5   Rest day
6   3 miles easy running
7   Houston-Tenneco Marathon
    3 hours 6 minutes 18 seconds

The 3-Hour 20-Minute Marathon

A 3-hour 20-minute marathon is attainable if you can run:

1 mile in 6 minutes
10K in 43 minutes 15 seconds

To run a 3-hour 20-minute marathon you need to average 7:38 per mile.

A ten-week base of 45 to 60 miles weekly is necessary before you begin the final ten-week countdown leading to the 3-hour 20-minute marathon. A typical week's training during this phase includes the following:

- one long stamina run of 12 to 15 miles at 8:00 to 9:00 per mile
- two track workouts, each consisting of the following:
  - 10 × 440 yards in 88 seconds, with a 660-yard recovery in between
  - 4 to 6 × 880 yards in 3 minutes 5 seconds to 3 minutes 15 seconds, with an 880-yard recovery in between
  - 3 × 1 mile in 6 minutes 20 seconds, with a 1-mile recovery in between
  - 2 × 2 miles in 13 minutes 10 seconds, with a 1.5-mile recovery in between
- four days of easy running (6 to 10 miles) at 8:00 to 9:00 per mile.

We will follow the fortunes of Bernie, a forty-three-year-old chiropractor, in his pursuit of this goal. Bernie has been running for most of his adult life and is a perfect example of an individual who truly loves to run. This particular characteristic has also been the dominant impediment to Bernie's improvement as a distance runner, because it has created the tendency to overrace throughout his career. (For this particular attempt Bernie has resolved to concentrate exclusively on preparing for the Tucson Marathon in order to achieve his goal.)

"Easy running" in this schedule is 8:00 to 9:00 per mile.

1st Week

Day

1 12 miles easy running
2 8 miles easy running
   incorporating 5 × 150 (fast and
   controlled)
3 8 miles easy running
   incorporating 6 miles in 46:00
4 10 miles easy running
5 10 × 220 in 45 — 440 R*
6 3 miles easy running
7 12 miles easy running

2nd Week

Day

1 18 miles in 2:15:00
2 10 miles easy running
3 8 × 440 in 95 — 440 R
4 9 miles easy running
5 10 miles easy running
   incorporating 6 miles in 43:00
6 15 miles easy running
7 12 miles easy running

3rd Week

Day

1 12 miles easy running
   incorporating 3 miles in 21:00
2 10 miles easy running
3 2 × 440 in 95 — 220 R; jog 880;
   2 × 1 mile in 6:20 — 660 R; jog
   880; 2 × 220 in 40 — 220 R
4 Rest day
5 6 miles easy running
   incorporating 2 miles in 13:00
6 Rest day
7 3 miles easy running

4th Week

Day

1 Phoenix Marathon (This was to be
   a long stamina run at
   approximately 8:00 per mile.
   Bernie, however, reverted to "type"
   and ran the entire distance in
   3:24:12, which translates into
   approximately 7:48 per mile.)
2 2 miles easy running
3 2 miles easy running
4 Rest day
5 Rest day
6 Rest day
7 6 miles easy running

5th Week

Day

1 8 miles easy running
2 10 miles easy running
3 6 miles easy running
4 8 miles easy running
5 6 miles easy running
   incorporating 2 miles in 14:00
6 12 miles easy running
7 Rest day

6th Week

Day

1 12 miles easy running
2 4 × 880 in 3:15 — 440 R
3 10 miles easy running
4 3 × 1 mile in 6:15 — 660 R
5 12 miles easy running
6 6 miles easy running
7 18 miles easy running

*Run 220 yards in 45 seconds, 10 times, with a 440-yard recovery in between.

7th Week

Day

1 15 miles easy running
   incorporating 6 miles in 42:00
2 9 miles easy running
3 5 × 1 mile in 6:30 — 440 R
4 Rest day
5 10 miles in 70:00
6 10 miles easy running
7 18 miles easy running

8th Week

Day

1 9 miles in 61:30
2 6 miles easy running
3 2 × 880 in 3:10 — 440 R; jog
   880; 2 miles in 12:30
4 9 miles easy running
   incorporating 6 miles in 42:00
5 15 miles easy running
6 6 miles easy running
7 18 miles easy running

9th Week

Day

1 15 miles easy running
2 9 miles easy running
3 5 × 880 in 3:05 — 660 R
4 10 miles easy running
5 15 miles easy running
   incorporating 9 miles in 63:00
6 6 miles easy running
7 15 miles easy running

10th Week

Day

1 12 miles easy running
2 7 miles easy running
   incorporating 2 × 1 mile in 6:20
3 6 miles easy running
4 Rest day
5 4 miles easy running
6 Rest day
7 Tucson Marathon
   3 hours 12 minutes 15 seconds

The 3-Hour 30-Minute Marathon

A 3-hour 30-minute marathon is attainable if you can run:

1 mile in 6 minutes 20 seconds
10K in 44 minutes 30 seconds

To run a 3-hour 30-minute marathon you need to average 7:59 per mile.

A ten-week base of 45 to 60 miles weekly is recommended before you begin the final ten weeks of specialized training leading to the 3-hour 30-minute marathon. A typical week's training during this period should consist of:

- one long stamina run of 10 to 15 miles at 8:30 to 9:30 per mile
- two track workouts with the emphasis on medium and long interval endurance training, each consisting of one of the following:
  - 10 × 440 yards in 92 to 95 seconds each, with a 440-yard recovery in between
  - 4 × 880 yards in 3 minutes 10 seconds to 3 minutes 20 seconds, with an 880-yard recovery in between
  - 3 × 1 mile in 6 minutes 45 seconds, with an 880-yard recovery in between
  - 2 × 2 miles in 13 minutes 30 seconds, with a 1-mile recovery in between
- four days of easy running (6 to 9 miles) at 8:30 to 9:30 per mile.

The 3-hour 30-minute marathon represents an important step in a runner's career. While many runners bypass this standard by beginning their marathon careers with faster initial clockings, for the majority of distance runners, the 3:30 clocking represents a formidable barrier. Now, for the first time, a runner must average below 8 minutes per mile for the distance, and many runners feel that an 8-minute average is the standard that separates the "plodder" from the "racer." While the authors hold that any runner who *completes* a marathon has attained "respectability," we also know from experience that running a 3:30 marathon is a very significant step in a distance runner's development.

We have included two schedules for this important time barrier. The left-hand schedule is the normal "optimum" schedule that has proved successful for the majority of my runners who have met the criteria described above. The right-hand schedule is a slightly modified version for Walter, a thirty-six-year-old attorney. These modifications are necessary since Walter, like several million Americans, is afflicted with sugar diabetes. Diagnosed as a diabetic at age seventeen, Walter has required daily insulin injections since 1965. He has completed four marathons since he began an endurance training program in 1982. His best marathon clocking is 3 hours 45 minutes.

Walter has been assisted in his ability to train since the introduction of a home glucose-monitoring program in July 1982. This has allowed him to test his own blood sugar with a glucometer in his home and office and to adjust his insulin intake accordingly. In the six months prior to this marathon attempt to break 3 hours 30 minutes, Walter has generally maintained an acceptable blood-sugar level through twice-a-day injections consisting of: before breakfast, 6 units of purified regular insulin (ACTRAPID) and 22 units of purified NPH insulin (PROTOPHANE), and before dinner, 6 units of ACTRAPID and 8 units of PROTOPHANE. Walter weighs 185 pounds. This is heavier than we would prefer a marathoner of his height (6′) to be, but in light of Walter's medical history we "have to dance with who brung us."

Walter's pre-race preparations are different from the average marathoner's in that he eats breakfast two hours before he races. During the course of the marathon he will consume two energy bars of approximately 200 calories each.

"Easy running" in both schedules is 8:30 to 9:40 per mile.

Optimum	**Walter**
1st Week	*1st Week*
Day	*Day*
1 12 miles easy running	1 10 miles easy running
2 8 miles easy running incorporating 4 × 880 in 3:10	2 8 × 440 in 92 — 440 R*
3 6 miles easy running incorporating 4 × 130 (fast and controlled)	3 7 miles easy running
4 8 miles easy running incorporating 5 miles in 39:00	4 4 × 880 in 3:10 — 880 R
5 8 × 220 in 46 — 440 R	5 7 miles easy running
6 3 miles easy running	6 3 miles easy running
7 12 miles easy running	7 12 miles easy running

*Run 440 yards in 92 seconds, 8 times, with a 440-yard recovery in between.

Optimum

2nd Week
Day

1. 15 miles in 2:03:45
2. 10 miles easy running
3. 16 × 110 in 22 — 110 R
4. 7 miles easy running
5. 10 miles easy running
   incorporating 6 miles in 45:00
6. 6 miles easy running
7. 15 miles easy running

3rd Week
Day

1. 12 miles easy running
   incorporating 3 miles in 21:00
2. 10 miles easy running
3. 3 × 1 mile in 6:45 — 440 R
4. 9 miles easy running
5. 7 miles easy running
   incorporating 5 miles in 36:00
6. 7 miles easy running
7. 12 miles easy running

4th Week
Day

1. 18 miles easy running
2. 10 × 220 in 46 — 220 R
3. 9 miles easy running
4. 6 miles easy running
   incorporating 3 miles in 20:30
5. 7 miles easy running
6. 5 miles easy running
7. 15 miles in 2:00:00

5th Week
Day

1. 15 miles easy running

2. 12 × 110 in 20 — 330 R
3. 9 miles easy running
4. 2 × 2 miles in 14:00 — 880 R
5. Rest day
6. 6 miles easy running
7. 18 miles in 2:24:00

Walter

2nd Week
Day

1. 9 miles easy running
2. 10 miles easy running
3. 2 × 1 mile in 6:30 — 880 R
4. 8 miles easy running
5. 6 miles easy running

6. 6 miles easy running
7. 15 miles easy running

3rd Week
Day

1. 12 miles in 96:00

2. 6 miles easy running
3. 10 × 440 in 92 — 220 R
4. 7 miles easy running
5. 15 miles easy running

6. Rest day
7. 12 miles easy running

4th Week
Day

1. 12 miles easy running
2. 7 miles easy running
3. 8 miles easy running
4. 4 × 880 in 3:10 — 660 R

5. 8 miles easy running
6. Rest day
7. 20 miles easy running

5th Week
Day

1. 10 miles easy running
   incorporating 3 miles in 22:00
2. 12 × 110 in 19 — 330 R
3. 6 miles easy running
4. 10 × 440 in 92 — 220 R
5. Rest day
6. 6 miles easy running
7. 12 miles in 90:00

Optimum	Walter

Optimum

6th Week

Day

1 12 miles easy running
2 4 × 880 in 3:20 — 660 R
3 8 miles easy running
4 3 × 1 mile in 6:40 — 660 R
5 10 miles easy running
6 3 miles easy running
7 21 miles easy running

7th Week

Day

1 12 miles easy running
   incorporating 6 miles in 42:00
2 6 miles easy running
3 10 × 220 in 46 — 220 R

4 6 miles easy running
5 10 miles in 75:00
6 10 miles easy running
7 18 miles easy running

8th Week

Day

1 12 miles easy running
   incorporating 3 miles in 20:30
2 5 miles easy running
3 4 × 1 mile in 6:45 — 660 R
4 6 miles easy running

5 10 miles in 75:00
6 3 miles easy running
7 15 miles in 1:52:30

9th Week

Day

1 15 miles easy running
2 6 miles easy running
3 5 × 880 in 3:15 — 660 R
4 9 miles easy running
5 10 miles in 75:00

Walter

6th Week

Day

1 9 miles easy running
2 8 × 220 in 40 — 440 R
3 7 miles easy running
4 4 × 880 in 3:06 — 440 R
5 6 miles easy running
6 4 miles easy running
7 30K Race: 2:19:45

7th Week

Day

1 6 miles easy running

2 6 miles easy running
3 6 miles easy running
   incorporating 1 mile in 7:00
4 2 × 1.5 miles in 9:45 — 880 R
5 7 miles easy running
6 6 miles easy running
7 18 miles easy running

8th Week

Day

1 10 miles easy running

2 4 × 1 mile in 6:15 — 660 R
3 7 miles easy running
4 2 miles in 13:30 — 880 R; 1 mile
   in 6:10 — 880 R; 880 in 3:00
5 Rest day
6 6 miles easy running
7 20 miles easy running

9th Week

Day

1 10 miles easy running
2 10 miles in 75:00
3 6 miles easy running
4 12 × 440 in 92 — 220 R
5 6 miles easy running

Optimum	**Walter**

9th Week (cont.)

Day

6 9 miles easy running
7 15 miles easy running

10th Week

Day

1 10 miles easy running
   incorporating 3 miles in 21:00
2 7 miles easy running
3 Rest day
4 6 miles easy running
5 Rest day
6 4 miles easy running
7 3-hour 30-minute marathon

9th Week (cont.)

Day

6 6 miles easy running
7 12 miles easy running
   incorporating 10 miles in 75:00

10th Week

Day

1 10 miles easy running

2 12 × 110 in 19 — 110 R
3 Rest day
4 2 × 1 mile in 6:30 — 880 R
5 Rest day
6 Rest day
7 4 miles easy running

11th Week

Day

1 Houston-Tenneco Marathon
   3 hours 38 minutes 10 seconds

Although Walter's training indicated that he was physically and mentally ready for his 3:30 marathon, he was unlucky in the weather for his race. The cold, wet conditions (38°F, 87% humidity) caused severe leg cramps that forced him to stop running several times. He finally had to change into full-length warmups in order to complete the race. In light of the time he lost to these complications, we felt that he had "morally" achieved his goal — and also illustrated the impact that poor running conditions can have on any marathoner, no matter how well trained.

Goldie (left)
Jackie (below)

The 3-Hour 45-Minute Marathon

A 3-hour 45-minute marathon is attainable if you can run:

1 mile in 6 minutes 45 seconds
10K in 47 minutes 30 seconds

To run a 3-hour 45-minute marathon you need to average
8:35 per mile.

A ten-week base of 40 to 55 miles weekly is necessary before you begin the final ten-week pre-marathon specialized training. A typical week should consist of:

- one long stamina run of 8 to 12 miles at 8:30 to 9:30 per mile
- two endurance workouts on the track, each consisting of one of the following:
  - 10 × 440 yards in 1 minute 40 seconds, with a 440-yard recovery in between
  - 4 to 6 × 880 yards in 3 minutes 30 seconds, with an 880-yard recovery in between
  - 4 × ¾ mile in 5 minutes 30 seconds, with an 880-yard recovery in between
  - 3 × 1 mile in 7 minutes 20 seconds, with an 880-yard recovery in between
- three days of easy runnng (5 to 7 miles) at 8:30 to 9:30 per mile
- one rest day OR another easy day of 5 to 7 miles at 8:30 to 9:30 per mile.

We will follow the progress of Goldie, a thirty-year-old librarian, and Jackie, a thirty-nine-year-old clinical social worker. Goldie and Jackie will both be attempting their first marathons. Goldie has been running for one year, while Jackie has been running for seven months. (Jackie was originally set for a 4-hour marathon, but her ten-week base work and lead-up races indicated that she could exceed the 4-hour barrier by a significant margin, and her schedule was adjusted accordingly.)

"Easy running" in both schedules is 8:30 to 9:30 per mile.

Goldie	Jackie

Goldie

1st Week

Day

1 12 miles easy running
2 3 × 880 in 3:30 — 880 R*
3 5 miles easy running
4 6 miles easy running
5 Rest day
6 3 miles easy running
7 15 miles in 2:05:00

2nd Week

Day

1 6 miles easy running
2 4 × 440 in 95 — 440 R
3 7 miles easy running
4 2 × 1 mile in 7:30 — 880 R
5 9 miles easy running
6 Rest day
7 15 miles easy running

3rd Week

Day

1 6 miles easy running
2 2 × 1 mile in 7:15 — 880 R
3 8 miles easy running
4 2 miles in 15:00
5 10 miles easy running
6 5 miles easy running
7 12 miles easy running

4th Week

Day

1 9 miles easy running
   incorporating 2 miles in 15:30
2 6 miles easy running
3 4 × 880 in 3:30 — 660 R
4 6 miles easy running

Jackie

1st Week

Day

1 13 miles easy running
2 3 × 880 in 3:30 — 880 R*
3 4 miles easy running
4 6 miles easy running
5 Rest day
6 3 miles easy running
7 25K race: 2:03:39**

2nd Week

Day

1 6 miles easy running
2 5 × 220 in 48 — 440 R
3 6 miles easy running
4 2 × 1 mile in 8:00 — 880 R
5 9 miles easy running
6 Rest day
7 15 miles easy running

3rd Week

Day

1 5 miles easy running
2 2 × 1 mile in 7:15 — 880 R**
3 7 miles easy running
4 1.5 miles in 10:30**
5 9 miles easy running
6 Rest day
7 10 miles easy running

4th Week

Day

1 10 miles easy running
   incorporating 2 × 1 mile in 7:20
2 10 × 110 in 20 — 330 R
3 6 miles easy running
4 1 mile in 7:45, ¾ mile in 5:40,
   880 in 3:25, 440 in 92 — all 660
   R**

*Run 880 yards in 3 minutes 30 seconds, 3 times, with an 880-yard recovery in between.

**The training and racing times indicated by ** on Jackie's schedule indicate that she could move up to more advanced training and could attempt a faster marathon pace than originally planned.

Goldie	Jackie

4th Week (cont.)

Day

	Goldie		Jackie
5	8 × 440 in 94 — 220 R	5	6 miles easy running
6	6 miles easy running	6	6 miles easy running
7	12 miles easy running	7	10 miles easy running

5th Week

Day

Goldie

1   6 miles easy running
2   3 × 220 in 48 — 220 R; 2 × 1 mile in 7:30 — 880 R
3   6 miles easy running

4   8 × 220 in 42 — 440 R

5   Rest day
6   4 miles easy running
7   ¼-marathon race: 50:13

Jackie

1   12 miles easy running
2   6 × 220 in 42 — 660 R

3   6 miles easy running incorporating 2 miles in 16:00
4   2 × 220 in 46, 2 × 440 in 95, 2 × 220 in 43 — all 440 R
5   Rest day
6   3 miles easy running
7   ¼-marathon race: 50:29**

6th Week

Day

Goldie

1   10 miles easy running
2   6 × 440 in 1:45 — 660 R
3   9 miles easy running
4   2 × 110 in 19 — jog 880; 2 miles in 15:30
5   Rest day
6   4 miles easy running
7   30K race: 2:44:30

Jackie

1   7 miles easy running
2   5 × 440 in 1:45 — 660 R
3   6 miles easy running
4   2 × 110 in 19 — jog 880; 2 miles in 15:30
5   Rest day
6   2 miles easy running
7   30K race: 2:44:44**

7th Week

Day

Goldie

1   6 miles easy running
2   6 × 440 in 1:45 — 440 R
3   3 miles easy running
4   5 miles easy running incorporating 2 miles in 15:30
5   6 miles easy running
6   12 miles easy running
7   9 miles easy running incorporating 4 miles in 32:00

Jackie

1   Rest day
2   3 miles easy running
3   6 miles easy running
4   4 × 220 in 50 — 660 R

5   5 miles easy running
6   3 miles easy running
7   15 miles easy running

Goldie	Jackie

Goldie

8th Week

Day

1 15 miles easy running
2 8 × 110 in 19 — 330 R
3 6 miles easy running
4 4 × 880 in 3:30 — 660 R
5 8 miles easy running
6 Rest day
7 18 miles easy running

9th Week

Day

1 10 miles easy running
   incorporating 3 miles in 23:00
2 6 miles easy running
3 8 × 440 in 92 — 440 R
4 6 miles easy running

5 2 × 1.5 miles in 11:30 — 880 R
6 Rest day
7 12 miles easy running
   incorporating 6 miles in 48:00

10th Week

Day

1 10 miles easy running
2 6 × 220 in 45 — 220 R
3 Rest day
4 6 miles easy running
5 Rest day
6 4 miles easy running
7 3 miles easy running

11th Week

Day

1 Houston-Tenneco Marathon
   3 hours 41 minutes 22 seconds

Jackie

8th Week

Day

1 6 miles easy running
2 4 × 880 in 3:40 — 880 R
3 6 miles easy running
4 2 × 1 mile in 7:20 — 880 R
5 8 miles easy running
6 Rest day
7 15 miles easy running

9th Week

Day

1 10 miles easy running

2 10 × 220 in 47 — 440 R
3 6 miles easy running
4 1 mile in 6:50, 880 in 3:15, 440 in
   87 — all 880 R
5 7 miles easy running
6 Rest day
7 12 miles easy running
   incorporating 5 miles in 40:00

10th Week

Day

1 10 miles easy running
2 Rest day
3 6 miles easy running
4 5 × 220 in 48 — 440 R
5 Rest day
6 3 miles easy running
7 Rest day

11th Week

Day

1 Houston-Tenneco Marathon
   3 hours 40 minutes 44 seconds

The 4-Hour Marathon

A 4-hour marathon is attainable if you can run:

1 mile in 7 minutes 15 seconds
10K in 50 minutes 30 seconds

To run a 4-hour marathon you need to average 9:10 per mile.

A ten-week base of 40 to 55 miles weekly is recommended before you begin the final ten-week pre-marathon specialized training. A typical week should consist of:

- one long stamina run of 8 to 12 miles at 9:00 to 10:00 per mile
- two endurance workouts on the track, each consisting of one of the following examples:
  - 8 to 10 × 110 yards in 22 seconds, with a 330-yard recovery in between
  - 6 to 8 × 220 yards in 45 to 48 seconds, with a 220- to 440-yard recovery in between
  - 4 to 6 × 440 yards in 96 seconds, with a 440-yard recovery in between
  - 2 to 4 × 880 yards in 3:45 to 4:00, with an 880-yard recovery in between
  - 2 × 1 mile in 7:45 to 8:00, with an 880-yard recovery in between
- three days of easy running (5 to 7 miles) at 9:00 to 10:00 per mile
- one rest day.

The subject in the training history below is Roy, a fifty-three-year-old energy exploration executive. Roy has been running for eighteen months and has already "survived" his first marathon. He is now concentrating on the "4-hour barrier," which represents a formidable obstacle in his progress as a distance runner.

Roy has successfully completed the ten-week foundation phase and during this time he occasionally raced in 10K "fun runs."

"Easy running" in this schedule is 9:00 to 10:00 per mile.

1st Week

Day

1. 15 miles in 2:15:00*
2. 3 × 220 in 47, 3 × 440 in 98, 2 × 110 in 21 — all 440 R**
3. 6 miles easy running
4. 2 × 220 in 45, 2 × 440 in 95, 2 × 880 in 3:45 — all 440 R
5. 8 miles easy running
6. Rest day
7. 13 miles easy running

2nd Week

Day

1. 13 miles easy running
2. 10 × 110 in 23 — 330 R
3. 6 miles easy running
4. 3 × 880 in 3:45 — 880 R
5. 13 miles easy running
6. Rest day
7. 15 miles easy running

3rd Week

Day

1. 10 miles easy running
2. 2 × 1 mile in 7:15 — 880 R*
3. 7 miles easy running
4. 1.5 miles in 10:30*
5. 3 miles easy running
6. Rest day
7. 15 miles in 2:11:15*

4th Week

Day

1. 6 miles easy running
2. 3 × 220 in 50, 880 in 3:45, 2 × 110 in 20 — all 660 R
3. 6 miles easy running
4. 4 × 110 in 22, 1.5 miles in 12:00, 2 × 220 in 43 — all 660 R
5. 6 miles easy running
6. 4 miles easy running
7. 10 miles easy running

5th Week

Day

1. 10 miles easy running incorporating 2 miles in 16:00*
2. 4 × 880 in 3:40 — 660 R
3. 7 miles easy running
4. 8 × 110 in 20 — 330 R
5. Rest day
6. 3 miles easy running
7. 19 miles in 2:46:15*

6th Week

Day

1. 4 miles easy running
2. 6 × 220 in 49 — 440 R
3. 7 miles easy running
4. 8 × 440 in 98 — 440 R
5. 10 miles easy running
6. 6 miles easy running
7. Rest day

*Workouts marked * are especially important as a gauge of the runner's progress, which needs to be more closely monitored at this level than at the level of the more elite athlete.

**Run 220 yards in 47 seconds, 3 times, with a 440-yard recovery in between; run 440 yards in 98 seconds, 3 times, with a 440-yard recovery in between; run 110 yards in 21 seconds, 2 times, with a 440-yard recovery in between.

7th Week

Day

1 12 miles easy running
2 3 × 220 in 45, 2 × 440 in 93, 2 × 220 in 43 — all 440 R
3 6 miles easy running
4 2 × 1 mile in 7:15 — 880 R*
5 10 miles easy running
6 Rest day
7 15 miles easy running

8th Week

Day

1 10 miles easy running incorporating 6 miles in 48:00*
2 6 × 110 in 20, 4 × 220 in 45 — all 330 R
3 6 miles easy running
4 3 miles in 21:30*
5 8 miles easy running
6 Rest day
7 20 miles easy running

9th Week

Day

1 10 miles easy running
2 10 × 220 in 47 — 440 R
3 6 miles easy running
4 1 mile in 6:50, 880 in 3:15, 440 in 87 — all 880 R*
5 7 miles easy running
6 Rest day
7 12 miles easy running

10th Week

Day

1 10 miles easy running
2 6 miles easy running
3 Rest day
4 6 miles easy running
5 Rest day
6 5 miles easy running
7 2 miles easy running

11th Week

Day

1 Tucson Marathon
   3 hours 50 minutes 14 seconds

The "Survival" Marathon

As running becomes more popular and, in particular, marathons receive more attention from the media, I am approached by a growing number of individuals who express an interest in running a marathon "one time only." Usually when I get their requests for assistance, the marathon is always just around the corner without an adequate period of time beforehand for the necessary foundation training for the event. Invariably, the aspiring distance runners will inform me that they are limited in their time to train ("I only have time to work out four or five times a week"); or that they are nursing old injuries ("I have this bad knee from playing football, baseball," etc.; or "I ran track once, but had to quit because of shin splints"). Generally, they will set a list of conditions: no lead-up racing prior to the marathon, and/or no track training, which ostensibly prevents the aggravation of their old injuries.

For several years I refused to work with this type of individual because I am philosophically opposed to "crash" programs in distance running. I feel that they have many negative aspects and that there is a good likelihood of incurring serious physical and physiological damage. I soon noted, however, that these individuals went ahead with their plans on their own, risking the consequences. Although I am not comfortable with the responsibility of coaching untested runners in the most demanding event in distance running, I eventually modified my approach and designed a "survival" marathon program — if the runners satisfied two major criteria:

- They had medical clearance to begin marathon training.
- They trained for a minimum of twelve weeks before their marathon attempt.

Most of the runners who fall into this category are just concerned with finishing the marathon distance before the official race clock is turned off — usually at 5 hours, which translates into an 11:25 per mile pace.

The most important difference between runners in the previous training examples and runners attempting to "survive" the marathon is that of tactical commitment. The former have time schedules and pacing guides to follow in their marathon attempt, while the "survival" group runs just to complete the distance and does not have any pressure to run certain time splits during the attempt. Both types of marathoner, however, must be thoroughly drilled on the very important distinction between "racing" and "finishing" a marathon. The "survival" marathoner also has the option of walking some portion of the marathon, should this become necessary.

"Easy running" in the "survival" marathon schedule is 11:00 to 12:00 per mile.

1st Week (5 days training only)

- 1 mile jog; 1 mile walk; 1 mile jog
- 2 miles jog
- 3 miles jog; 1 mile walk; 2 miles jog
- 4 miles jog
- 4 miles jog; 1 mile walk; 2 miles jog

2nd Week (5 days training only)

- 6 miles jog
- 3 miles jog; 1 mile walk; 3 miles jog
- 4 miles jog; 1 mile walk; 1 mile easy running
- 5 miles easy running
- 6 miles easy running incorporating 2 miles in 20:00

3rd Week (5 days training only)

- 5 miles easy running
- 3 miles easy running
- 9 miles easy running
- 6 miles easy running
- 6 miles easy running incorporating 3 miles in 30:00

4th Week (5 days training only)

- 3 miles easy running
- 9 miles easy running
- 3 miles easy running incorporating 2 miles in 20:00
- 7 miles easy running
- 8 miles easy running

5th Week (5 days training only)

- 6 miles in 60:00
- 3 miles easy running
- 10 miles easy running
- 7 miles easy running incorporating 5 miles at *best-effort* pace
- 5 miles easy running

6th Week (5 days training only)

- 4 miles easy running
- 10 miles easy running
- 9 miles easy running incorporating 3 miles at *best-effort* pace
- 6 miles easy running incorporating 2 3-minute intervals at *best-effort* pace
- 5 miles easy running

7th Week (5 days training only)

- 12 miles easy running
- 5 miles easy running
- 4 miles easy running
- 10 miles in 1:40:00 (10:00 per mile pace)
- 7 miles easy running

8th Week (6 days training)

- 6 miles easy running
- 16 miles (just to complete the distance)
- 3 miles easy running incorporating 4 × 110 (fast and controlled)
- 8 miles easy running
- 5 miles easy running incorporating 3 miles in 30:00
- 7 miles easy running

9th Week (6 days training)

- 3 miles easy running
- 12 miles easy running
- 9 miles easy running incorporating 6 miles in 60:00
- 6 miles easy running
- 10 miles easy running
- 7 miles easy running

10th Week (6 days training)

- 5 miles easy running
- 16 miles easy running
- 10 miles easy running
- 6 miles easy running incorporating 3 miles at *best-effort* pace
- 3 miles easy running incorporating 4 × 110 (fast and controlled)
- 5 miles easy running

11th Week (5 days training)

- 13 miles easy running
- 6 miles easy running incorporating 3 miles in 30:00
- 8 miles easy running
- 5 miles easy running
- 10 miles in 1:40:00 (10:00 per mile pace)

12th Week (4 days training)

- 8 miles easy running
- 6 miles easy running incorporating 2 miles in 20:00
- 4 miles easy running
- 3 miles easy running
- "Survival" marathon attempt

EIGHT

Backgrounds

IN THIS CHAPTER, we answer some of the questions frequently asked by beginning runners.

Q. *I'm just beginning to think about running competitively. How do I begin? How soon can I race? Do you think I can run a marathon this year?*

A. The traditional advice is: if you have not been running at all, see a doctor to find out whether you have any pre-existing condition that would make running harmful to you. This is good advice, especially if you're over thirty.

You will be ready to race a 10K when you can run about 20 miles a week for five to six weeks in a row without injury.

The answer to the marathon question is "probably." You can plan on finishing a marathon — jogging through it — if you can hold to 35 to 40 miles a week for ten weeks prior to the marathon. (See the "survival" schedules for more information.)

Q. *I've been doing all my running on the streets. Your schedules call for 440's, 880's, and so on, and I'm not sure exactly what they mean.*

A. The normal outdoor track is 440 yards or 400 meters (the two distances are almost the same). A 220 is half the way around the track; a 110 is one-fourth the way around; and 880 is twice around. (A 440 is sometimes called a quarter, because it's a quarter-mile; an 880 is a half.) On most tracks there are marks painted on the surface, or markers by the rail, to indicate the 220 and 110's.

Indoor tracks pose a bit more of a problem: some are 200 meters long (about 8 laps to the mile), others are 11 or 15 laps to the mile, depending on the space that was available when they were built. If you run on a track like this, ask someone to show you where the interval marks are.

Q. *Will coffee help me race better?*
A. Caffeine has been shown to improve the capacity for work, although evidence suggests that its long-term use may cause health problems. Also, some runners have trouble with the acidity of coffee, so try it before a workout.

Q. *Should I eat a candy bar before I race?*
A. Probably not. Theophylline and theobromine act like caffeine, and both are present in chocolate. (A racehorse has been disqualified after winning after it had eaten a candy bar.) And the sugar, instead of acting to increase your energy level, will probably trigger an insulin overproduction and a blood sugar decrease. Forget the candy bar.

Q. *What about drinking alcohol and running?*
A. You should always stop running while drinking, otherwise you'll spill. Most runners of our acquaintance drink a beer or a glass of wine occasionally, but I doubt if any of them think it helps them run faster. Most runners who are very serious — aiming at the Olympic trials or a national championship — will skip alcohol entirely until after the meet.

For endurance runners, alcohol has some bad side effects — first, it is dehydrating, so it can lead to heat-related injury; second, it affects the body's "thermostat" (the mechanism which controls the body's ability to sense and regulate its temperature) again leading to heat-related problems. (If you've awakened in the middle of the night hot and dry after too many beers, you've seen these effects of excessive alcohol.) Such problems may be compounded by the fact that endurance training tends to reduce the percentage of fat in the body, reducing one's alcohol tolerance — that is, it doesn't take as much alcohol to be too much as it used to.

Q. *Can I run with a hangover?*
A. Running can help you get rid of a hangover. The first mile will be the worst, and then it will get easier. Be sure to drink early and often during the workout (water, that is) because alcohol in large quantities is very dehydrating.

Q. *I'm running my first race in a week. Should I carbo-load?*
A. No. For any distance under 30K (18.6 miles) carbo-loading won't do any good at all. If it's a first marathon you're running, you don't want to

make experiments like carbo-loading. Change your routines as little as possible from what you do in training.

For later races, you may want to try either the "classic" carbo-loading techniques — a 20-mile run one week before, followed by three days of depletion (nothing but fats and proteins), then three days of loading (three days of a heavy carbohydrate diet) — or the modified form in which the depletion stage is eliminated. In any case, the psychological and physical benefits of carbo-loading need to be balanced against the fact that there are some medical reports of adverse consequences. You will also feel "stuffed" all over because your body stores four times as much water as glycogen, and you will feel heavy and slow for the first two-thirds of the race. Most important, never assume you can substitute any diet for doing the training.

Q. What should a marathoner in training eat?
A. First, whatever he's hungry for, and second, enough. Many runners look for the magic diet that will suddenly bring them into great racing shape, but it doesn't exist. Too many runners take the other road, too, trying to diet themselves down to 2 percent body fat so they'll "run lighter." Usually they get weak faster than they get light; additionally, there is a real danger in low body-fat levels — runners have died from cardiac problems apparently triggered by low body fat. If you're running regularly, you need to eat about 100 calories per mile extra just to maintain your weight.

Q. Should runners take extra vitamins?
A. Most studies show that normal sedentary people don't need vitamin supplements; endurance runners, of course, aren't sedentary, and many people don't think they're normal either. Most runners assume that they need extra vitamins and minerals and take such a supplement. Many of our acquaintances also feel that extra vitamins C and E help prevent soreness.

Q. I'm a little overweight. What effect will that have on my running?
A. It will affect it, of course. Obviously, the more you weigh, the more your legs have to work. Furthermore, your heart has to work extra hard to pump blood through the excess fat, and your lungs have to supply it with oxygen. In endurance running, all this means that your limit will be lower than it would be if you weren't carrying the extra weight around. It is often amazing, however, to see how well some heavyset people run. In any case, the training you do will help you burn off approximately

100 calories per mile. That doesn't seem like much, but it can add up. Running can also help you stay on a diet. When you realize that you'd need to run an extra 15 miles to make up for that tasty-looking pizza, somehow "15 miles" has a reality to it that 1500 calories may lack.

Q. *What is my ideal running weight, anyway?*
A. There's an old rule of thumb that your weight in pounds should be twice your height in inches — so if you're 5'10", you "should" weigh 140. This is unrealistic for most runners. Among long-distance specialists, weights vary — for example, steeplechaser Henry Marsh is 5'10", weighs 160 pounds, and has been ranked number one in the world. Mary Decker, 1500-meter and 3000-meter world champion, is 5'7" and weighs 112, while Jarmila Kratochvilova, a 400- and 800-meter world-record holder, is 5'7" and weighs 148. You should not try to get your body fat down to extremely low levels. Your body will pick its own weight if you keep your training consistent.

Q. *What kind of shoes should I wear on the track?*
A. You can wear the same shoes that you wear on the roads and trails. You don't need to buy a pair of spikes unless you are racing short distances (up to 880 yards), or unless the track is so loose that you slip around even at training pace. The main thing to avoid in running shoes for the track is weight: not only do heavy shoes slow you down, but they predispose you to injury if you try to run intervals in them.

Q. *My shoes smell.*
A. So do ours.

Q. *How should you take care of shoes to make sure they last?*
A. Shoes used to wear out first on the sole. That seems to have been overcome by high-carbon rubber in shoe soles. Now shoes usually fall apart first. The best way to help them seems to be (1) brush them if they're dry and dirty; (2) rinse them with cold water if you've sweated through them, and stuff them with newspapers to dry; (3) don't wear the same pair several days in a row. With this treatment, shoes will usually last three to four months. Don't put them in a dryer or leave them in a hot car; the soles and midsoles may separate.

Q. *I have a pair of shoes that I don't run in much; they're a year old and are still in good condition, even the soles. Now that I'm going to start serious training, will they be all right?*
A. Unfortunately, no, probably not. The curing process that hardens the rubber in running shoes does not stop when the shoe is shipped from

the factory; it continues, making the sole harder and harder, and thus progressively decreasing the shock absorption of the shoe. By the time a running shoe is four months old, in most cases a lot of its cushioning is gone, and the risk of injury is increased.

Q. *What if it's raining when I'm supposed to do my workout?*
A. Some runners take rainy days off. They are missing out on a good thing. Rain is usually uncomfortable only for the first mile or so; then the body warms up enough so that it feels good — or at the worst, fairly good. One thing to watch on rainy days is the surface you're on. Wet roads and wet tracks can get slippery, increasing your chance of injury, while dirt and grass get muddy and soft, with the same result. Your shoes also get heavier. So a fast track workout is too dangerous, but usually rain is ideal for long endurance work. The cooling effect of the rain actually makes that kind of workout easier.

Q. *Can I run with a cold?*
A. Usually, if it's a mild one. If you have a fever, though, you should wait at least 24 hours after the fever leaves before you run. If you don't have a fever, running may help you get over your cold. It has been suggested that the slightly elevated body temperatures running causes mimic the fever, which is a defense mechanism of the body. The adrenaline you release when you run will help overcome some of a cold's symptoms, like congestion. In summary, running may cause you to have fewer colds than you did before you started running. If you get several in a row, it's nearly always a sign that you're overtraining (or are under unusual stress from some other cause — job, family, and so forth). See Chapter 5.

Q. *I've had diarrhea in two marathons. What can I do?*
A. Several things can cause that problem. A small percentage of runners cannot handle milk and milk products. Even more have trouble with fresh fruits and vegetables they've eaten a day or two before the race. Sometimes the race directors, in an attempt to help you out, will mix the replacement drinks too strong, and high sugar and stress may combine to produce diarrhea. Drink water during the race itself, replacement drinks afterward.

Q. *I travel a lot — how can I get my training in?*
A. First, make sure that you get the more important runs taken care of. If you're a marathoner, the strength run is the most important single workout, followed by the track training. If you're racing 10K's, the order

is reversed: track work first, then strength run. In any case, do as much of this kind of work as you can on a familiar track or road course; juggle your schedule around to permit it. But don't do two or three hard days in a row, of course.

Having done that (as much as possible), the other four days of the week are easy running, which you can do almost anywhere. If you're in a strange city, do the old "out and back" from your hotel (take some money for cab fare in case you get lost). In an airport, you may have two hours between flights. Rent a locker, change clothes, and get eight or ten miles in, shower, and catch your flight. You'll probably feel a lot better than if you just sit around the airport.

Q. Do those altitude simulators — those scuba-tank things — really help?
A. I don't see how they can do much good. You only wear them for an hour or two while you run, and even if you move to a higher altitude, it takes weeks and months and years before runners receive significant benefits. I also am hesitant about anything that affects your running style when you wear it. Many times, runners look for an extra edge to give them improved performance. That's fine, as long as you don't think that whatever you use to get your edge — weights, or bicycling, or vitamins, or bee pollen, or whatever you believe works for you — gives you a short cut so you can avoid doing the training. You can't.

Q. How do you handle the monotony of a long run?
A. There are a number of ways. I always think of a workout as going over a hill — when I reach halfway it's "all downhill" from here. If I can get halfway, I believe I've got it beaten. And of course, getting in the psychological groove of finishing all your workouts makes it easier to finish the hard ones you'll have later.

Q. What about those portable tape players to help relieve boredom?
A. I don't think they're a good idea. If you are purely a recreational runner, or jog for your health, then maybe it won't matter, but I think that even the lightest versions can pull your form off.

Q. Any thoughts on running clothes?
A. There are practical considerations, of course. Wear something that is appropriate for the weather. Don't wear anything brand new in a long race like a marathon; wear it in a training run first to make sure it doesn't bind or chafe.

There are interesting psychological aspects to the clothes you wear while racing, too. Although a lot of competitive runners scoff at the novices who show up at the starting line in $400 worth of warmups, I do believe that you'll run better in real running shorts and a top than in a pair of cut-offs and a T-shirt. Looking like a runner helps you to become one. Even when I was racing at the international level, I always made sure that my running shorts were ironed — something my old Australian coach taught me. So it's not just the herd instinct at work, but also a sense of self-image. That can affect your racing a lot.

Q. *What about weight training for runners?*
A. It's probably only marginally useful for distance runners, although sprinters use it a lot. Psychologically, it can help you feel stronger, and that may help you race better. Avoid exercises that build a lot of bulk, like using very heavy weights with only a few repetitions. Light weights and many repetitions build strength without too much bulk. Concentrate on shoulders, upper arms, and chest. Some runners who don't get to the gym very often find that a portable typewriter gives them a good workout. Also, runners should do bent-leg situps to strengthen their abdominal muscles.

Q. *I've been coaching myself for several years, and now I've joined a running club that has a coach with a good deal of experience. Do you have any advice for runners being coached for the first time?*
A. First, make a commitment. Your coach is going to be spending time and thought trying to help you realize your potential. Don't shrug off his suggestions. Discuss them with him if you don't understand why he wants you to do a particular workout.

Second, don't expect miracles. If you've been doing all of your running on roads and trails, and he moves you to the track twice a week, it may take a year for your body to make the adjustment and for your times to start improving.

Third is a bit of advice I give all my runners: NEVER pass your coach in a race.

One from the Ranks

RUNNERS AT THE INTERNATIONAL LEVEL have an expression they use when discussing the expected outcome of an upcoming race; after all the obvious favorites are mentioned, someone is sure to add, "And there's always one from the ranks." And it's nearly always true: someone who has never distinguished himself or herself as a racer will suddenly come to the fore, as the months and years of consistent training pay off. Marianne Dickerson's silver medal in the marathon at the Helsinki World Championships in 1983 is a good recent example, while — as this chapter was being written — Geoff Smith of England led the New York Marathon for twenty-six miles, ensuring that he could never be classed as an "unknown" again.

Time after time, a similar phenomenon has happened to the athletes who train using the schedules and philosophies in this book. They may have been only mediocre in sports before — in a few cases, they had no sports background at all — but with consistent application to the training, they have become the winners of local races, national age-group medalists, and even American- and world-record holders.

The purpose of this book is to enable you to "come up," to improve your running, to make you as good a runner as you can be.

Don't be afraid to let it work. Choose a realistic goal, do the training, run smart — and take a few chances. Remember, there's always "one from the ranks."

Why shouldn't that one be you?

INDEX

Photograph Acknowledgments

Pages 2, 14, 60, 78, 94, 110, 113, 129, 164, 168, 178, 192, 200, photos by Mark Scheid.

Page 23, photo by Fred Bunch. With permission of *The Houston Post*.

Page 29 left, photo courtesy of Marathon Foto.

Pages 29 right, 98, 172, 192 left, 212, photos by Lynn C. Trafton.

Page 34, from collection of Allan Lawrence. Reproduced courtesy Australian Consolidated Press.

Page 44, from collection of Dr. Herbert L. Fred. With permission of *The Honolulu Advertiser*.

Page 68, from collection of Allan Lawrence.

Page 75, from collection of Pat Clohessy.

Page 106, photo by Doug Feld.

Page 118, photo by Phil Baker.

Page 124, photo by Tim Jewett, *The Oregonian*, Portland, Oregon.

Page 132, photo by Harris Masterson III.

Page 134, photo by Becky Raine.

Pages 160, 186, photos by Sport Photo.

Page 182, photo by Bernie Finch.

Page 204, photo by Mike Fred.